Harvey Couch

Harvey Couch

An Entrepreneur Brings Electricity to Arkansas

Stephen Wilson

August House / Little Rock
P U B L I S H E R S

Printed in the United States of America
10 9 8 7 6 5 4 3 2 1
LIBRARY OF CONGRESS CATALOGING-IN-PUBLICATION DATA
Harvey Couch: An Entrepreneur Brings Electricity to Arkansas.
Wilson, Stephen, 1954-
Harvey Couch.
Includes index.
1. Couch, Harvey Crowley, 1877-1941.
2. Arkansas Power & Light Company—History.
3. Businessmen—United States—Biography.
4. Electric utilities—Arkansas—History.
5. Railroads—United States—History.
6. Reconstruction Finance Corporation—History.
I. Title
HD9685.U5C678   1986   363.6'2'09767   86-22323
ISBN 0-87483-025-7 (alk. paper)
ISBN 0-87483-026-5 (leather : alk. paper)

First Edition, 1986

Production artwork by Byron Taylor
Typography by Lettergraphics, Little Rock, AR
Design direction by Ted Parkhurst
Project direction by Hope Coulter

This book is printed on archival-quality paper which meets the guidelines
for performance and durability of the Committee on Production Guidelines
for Book Longevity of the Council on Library Resources.

AUGUST HOUSE, INC. PUBLISHERS LITTLE ROCK

Acknowledgements

The author would like to make grateful acknowledgement of the following sources which provided the bulk of the background material for this book: the corporate files of Arkansas Power and Light, containing Harvey Couch's personal scrapbooks and many old photographs; the Pratt Remmel family; Mr. William Couch; the microfilm section of the Central Arkansas Library System; and the Winter 1984 issue of the *Arkansas Historical Quarterly* for its summary of the 1927 flood in an article by Russell Bearden.

S.W.

For Diane

Chapter One

Tom Couch was wild. Everyone in Calhoun, Arkansas, said so. Driving his horse and buggy at all kinds of speeds, staying out late at night, he seemed out of control. He was loud, too. He was always surrounded by a rowdy gang of boys. People said you heard Tom coming down the street before you saw him. Calhoun was a small town and everyone knew that Tom's father, Quincy Couch, had all but sat on him to hold him down, but it was no use. The whole town agreed, at seventeen, Tom was a boy well on his way to being "no good."

Quincy Couch was the first Democratic sheriff in Columbia County since the end of Reconstruction. He had enough to worry about without having to police his own son. But Tom was a problem that did not seem to have an answer. Quincy had seen a lot of the world—he had driven a horse and wagon across most of the United States, served with the South in the Civil War, and as sheriff had seen both the good and bad in people—but nothing in his experience had prepared him to deal with a boy who did not want anything from life.

The kinds of trouble that anyone could get into in a town of eight hundred people were limited, but as Tom had grown older, Quincy's fears had increased. Of course, there was the ever-present temptation of moonshine liquor. But even more frightening, many young men were leaving home via northbound freights to try their luck in the industrialized northern cities, and whether they fared better or worse most never returned. It seemed only a matter of time before Tom joined them.

Manie Heard was not the girl for Tom Couch. Quiet and shy, she had recently moved to Calhoun with her widowed mother. At Calhoun's general store, where most folks gathered during the day, they knew she did not realize that Tom was a boy to be avoided. It was the duty of each of them to warn her. "Stay away from him," they said, in every different way they could, but it was no use. Manie refused to stop seeing Tom. She saw something very special in him and believed he could be anything he wanted. No one, not even Tom, could shake that belief. Quiet, shy Manie had a will of iron. Each day they would sit together and talk about what a young man who wanted to settle down could do with his life. Purpose and ambition lead to accomplishment, she told him. The measure of a man's life rested on what he did with what he had. Manie believed this more than anything: a constructive life was the kind God intended. As time passed Tom learned much about Manie, himself, and what he wanted to do with his life. Manie's quiet convictions worked a change in him. Four years later, she and the ex-troublemaker, now Methodist minister, were married. Quincy Couch had seen nothing like it.

The Couches were farmers. As far back as anyone could remember the Couch family had made their living from the soil, first in Georgia, and after Tom's father and uncles had moved to Calhoun in 1851, in Arkansas. After Manie and Tom were married it was expected that they would go to work on the family farm. They did. Tom also traveled each Sunday to different towns near Calhoun to preach. At first their life was everything they could have hoped. The reformed Tom and his young wife were popular. On weekends the farm was filled with their friends from town. The ladies gathered for a quilting bee in the parlor while the men held informal shooting matches out back. Children and dogs, meanwhile, ran noisily back and forth between the groups.

Trouble soon came to the farm. Cotton was still king in the South, and though it was considered a cash crop by the banks, it was a cash crop that made its growers earn every penny. Planting, weeding, and harvesting 130 acres in the hot Arkansas sun were beginning to take its toll on what was turning out to be the fragile health of Tom.

The solution was a family. The farms of America in the nineteenth century depended upon the division of labor that large families provided. On August 21, 1877, the first of six children was born to the Couches. They named him Harvey Crowley Couch, and as he grew he, and later his three younger brothers and two sisters, would take their place beside their father in the fields. Anyone who took the time to think about it might have assumed that young Harvey would one day be a farmer like generations of the Couch family before him, but almost from the first this boy had other ideas.

If nothing else, Harvey Couch was getting a full picture of life on a farm. His earliest memories would be of the morning chores, followed by the afternoon chores and finally the night-time chores. The only breaks in routine came each Sunday and during the two months each year when special classes were held for children of farmers. These classes taught a pupil how to read and write but did not attempt to inspire the mind. William McKay, the town's schoolteacher, did not believe that the mind needed to be inspired to perform farm labors. To him, picking cotton was an education in itself. It was probably natural that while Harvey's body was occupied with his daily chores, or patiently sitting through two months of "reading, 'riting, and 'rithmetic" each year, his mind would yearn for something to combat the monotony. He was more than ready for something new and different to think about. At a young age Harvey discovered that something new. It was the world of machines.

At that time Thomas Edison had only recently lit his laboratory in Menlo Park; Henry Ford was just beginning to fiddle with the internal combustion engine. The McCormick reaper had introduced mechanical harvesting in the Midwest, but in the South, cotton was still a hand-picked crop. The Arkansas farm of the 1880s was one of horses and plows, pitchforks and hoes, sore muscles and sweat. To rural people like the Couches machines were truly part of another world—as foreign to small farms as anything could be.

On a trip to Hope, about fifty miles from Calhoun, Harvey came face to face with his first complex machine. Tom decided to stop their wagon at a rail crossing to show Harvey the greatest machine of nineteenth-century America—the locomotive. From the time he saw the small puffs of smoke approaching in the distance, Harvey knew he was on to something. As the train approached ever closer, he felt as if he might explode with excitement. The very ground beneath them was shaking! "It's the Cotton Belt," Tom shouted. The faint rumble was now a roar. Then it was upon them, with its whistle blowing, wheels churning, and cinders spitting. It made the horses buck. But what power! What speed! This was quite a machine. After the earth had stopped trembling, Tom prodded the horses over the track and on toward the cotton gin at Hope. Everything was returning to normal—except Harvey. He stared after the retreating train until it could no longer be seen in the distance.

Back at home, Harvey found the farm unbearably quiet. He kept thinking about the train, what it must be like to ride on one, to harness all that power and glide across the countryside. The world of the future was the world of machines and trains, and he could not wait to be a part of the future. One day he must own a train. But that would not satisfy him today. Almost instinctively, Harvey set out to recreate a smaller version of that locomotive for himself. He did not have an inventive mind, but he was forming a kinship with machines that would focus all his attention on them, and he needed to understand them inside and out. He set about gathering scrap material for his new Couch Express. Siding from an old barn, fence rails, tin roofing—anything and everything was used for the new railroad.

First, he laid split timber down the side of a hill to form a kind of track. He cut tree stumps to provide round (sort of) wheels for his soon-to-be train. For the train car, he made a platform of discarded lumber and an old door. He added a cowbell to simulate the whistle of the train. He connected the wheels. His father took an old bucket of whitewash and painted "Cotton Belt" on the side of the vehicle. The Couch Express was ready.

Harvey summoned his mother to witness the maiden voyage, set his contraption between the tracks, and pushed off. The train rushed down the hill, with Harvey barely hanging on, until it stopped with a thud at the bottom. He rolled off the platform laughing.

"Did you see that?" he called up to his mother.

"Yes, I sure did," she answered. She smiled at his enthusiasm but wondered what all this was about. During the remainder of the day she would hear the train many more times as, with its cowbell clanging and Couch cheering, it bumped down the hillside. At dusk Manie forced Harvey to abandon his engineer duties until the next day.

When morning finally came, Harvey flew through his chores. He had a train to run. An idea was worth nothing unless it was developed, Harvey thought. The next step in the development of his train would be to add a steaming boiler to the Express. That was what made the real trains go. He mounted a small tin drum on the platform and built a coal fire underneath. He added water and then sealed the lid and waited for something to happen.

Something happened quite shortly. The drum exploded with a wallop that sent Couch sailing through the air. He landed in some bushes, unhurt. Machines surely were powerful—but perhaps they needed more study.

Harvey grew in feet as other people grew in inches. While still a young boy he was almost as big as his father. As his father's health continued to fail, he took on a bigger responsibility for the farm. He rarely had the opportunity to attend the short farm classes, although his parents insisted that he go whenever possible. His world now was limited to the farm. This isolation from other people made him sometimes seem shy and backward with strangers. Among the members of his own family and friends, however, there was no one more straightforward and dependable than Harvey.

Shyness did not stop him from speaking up when there was something he wanted. A local merchant was selling a pair of guineas. Like every farm boy his age, Harvey wanted a set for himself to breed and trade. But there was one problem—money. Tom Couch needed every dime that he or the children earned to support his large family. There was no money for anything but the necessities, certainly not for a pair of guinea birds. Harvey understood the family's need, but he was determined that he would not be denied. There must be a way to get what you want without always depending on money, he thought. Some sort of trade seemed to be called for, but Harvey had nothing to trade that the merchant would value. He had one possibility in mind— but it would require some tall talking. One afternoon he finished his chores early and walked purposefully into town. He paced in front of the store, gathering his courage. He took a deep breath, walked into the general store, and headed straight for the high counter at the rear.

"Good morning, Mr. Stone. I'd like to see that pair of guineas you have in the window."

"Well, sure, Harvey. They're pretty, aren't they?"

Stone crossed back to the window and fetched the birds.

"Good, strong birds," Stone said. "Do you want them, Harvey?—only 50 cents for the pair."

Harvey braced himself. He hoped this sounded as good as when he had practiced it.

"Yes, sir, I sure do, but only if you'll let me pay you twice that amount."

"What's that?" The old man tried to focus his glasses on the gangling youth in front of him.

"I'll be honest with you, Mr. Stone. I don't have the money for these birds. But if you'll let me take them now I'll pay you twice their worth in guinea eggs."

Stone studied Harvey's face for a moment. Guinea eggs were always in demand. Stone smiled. "Let's sit down for a minute, Harvey. I didn't know you were a horse trader."

An hour later, Harvey was on his way home with two birds in hand. He was excited to have his birds at last but he also felt a strong sense of pride that he was able to sell himself to Mr. Stone.

Over the next few weeks he kept a eye on their guinea hen. He wanted to make sure that he repaid Mr. Stone as soon as possible. One evening the first eggs were laid. Harvey counted the batch—six eggs. He would be well on his way to guinea egg solvency. The next morning he went to the nest, planning to gather the eggs and take them into town. He stopped short at the nest. The eggs were gone. Harvey couldn't believe his eyes. He heard a noise behind him and turned. It was a long grey snake with six egg-shaped bulges down its length. Now he knew where the eggs were, and he could not lose those eggs. Harvey ran to the woodpile and grabbed the axe. He raced back in time to see the snake slither down the edge of a slope toward some tangled undergrowth behind the barn. Harvey slid down after it, dropping the axe as he slid, and scrambling to pick it back up. Without stopping to dust himself off, Harvey began to stalk the egg-filled snake. At first he couldn't find it; then a movement in the weeds to his right caught his eye. It was the snake sliding quickly away from him. Another second and it would be gone for good. Harvey lumbered after it and caught it just as it was going under a bush. He grabbed the tail and brought the axe down on its head. The snake began to jerk violently, and Harvey held it down until it died. He then took a knife out of his pocket, split the snake down the middle, gently pried the eggs out, and bundled them in his handkerchief. He took them over to the pump to wash them and examined them for damage. They were all right. He immediately took them to town. More than ever determined to be as good as his word, Harvey became mother hen to the mother hen. He would watch carefully over her to insure she was safe. She became his first responsibility in the morning and his last stop at night. After several more hatchings the guineas were paid for.

It was becoming apparent that the farm troubles were not going to be temporary. Tom's health was getting steadily worse. The summers brought fever and the winters were worse. To help bolster the farm's income, Harvey took his first job off the farm. Naturally, it involved machinery.

The local cotton gin used a steam engine to process the raw cotton. They needed a boy to arrive before work and begin the tedious process of firing up the boiler. This involved stoking the boiler with heavy, four-foot logs. It was a physically demanding job. But it paid the princely sum of 50 cents a day, and to Harvey it bore great excitement and responsibility. Actually being the person to bring this huge boiler up to pressure was thrilling. Each morning he would watch the gauges climb toward full pressure and feel pride in the power he commanded. Each evening he stayed to quiet the fire in the belly of this great machine. This wasn't work! This was what it must be like to command a steam locomotive. If he had the money he would pay for this opportunity.

When the end of the farm finally came, it was almost anti-climactic. Manie and Tom had tried everything they could to save it. More and more of the decisions were now being made by Manie as Tom's health continued to fail. Even the younger children knew something was wrong, and when Tom and Manie told them they were finally giving up, they were not surprised. They would be moving to nearby Magnolia, the county seat.

Magnolia had been created when Columbia County was formed in 1853. The townspeople of Calhoun had resented the slight to their older town, but what was done was done. Magnolia was now the town of the future. Calhoun had a population of only 806, while the new town of Magnolia had already climbed to over 1,500. There would be more opportunities in Magnolia, its citizens told the Couches—everything would be fine. Manie could teach music and the children could find odd jobs in town. In the next few days Harvey helped his father sell items they wouldn't be needing in town. He had mixed feelings about the move: he knew he never would want to be a farmer, but he did not know what life would be like in a big place like Magnolia.

Seventeen-year-old Harvey Couch stood across the dirt road from the Magnolia schoolhouse and tried to imagine what a full year in school would be like. This would be the first time Harvey met the children of his new hometown. Manie had been excited that he would finally be able to get a standard education instead .of the two-month farm classes. Harvey wasn't so sure. Because of his lack of education he had been placed with students twelve and thirteen years old. Harvey didn't know how they would take to a new, older kid in school. As soon as he walked into the noisy classroom he found out. One by one the students nudged each other and turned to gape with open mouths at his looming figure.

Harvey was now six feet tall. Years of farm living and work at the cotton gin had added to his massive frame. He towered above everyone else in the classroom. After the boys of the class had taken a few careful moments to size up the extent of his amiability, they began to make life miserable for this natural target, an awkward, oversized farm boy in a hickory shirt and overalls. Unintentionally, Harvey had galvanized the class into two separate groups: Harvey Couch and everyone else.

At first Harvey took the taunts with his characteristic good nature. But as the ridicule continued over the weeks, he became very quiet amid the activity of the room.

Pat Neff was the young teacher in charge of the class. He was aware of the taunts and jokes made at Harvey's expense but did not know quite how to handle them. As he saw Harvey grow more and more withdrawn he realized he must take some sort of action. He asked Harvey to remain after class one day.

"What's going on with you, Harvey?" Neff inquired.

"I don't know. I guess I don't fit in. I've been thinking about dropping out, going to work," Harvey mumbled.

Neff nodded. He crossed over to the blackboard and wrote, "A quitter never wins and a winner never quits." Couch stared blankly at the words. Neff crossed in front of his desk and sat down beside Harvey. He then began to speak about possibilities for Harvey's future, possibilities that would depend on an education. He began to lay out a plan of action for the boy. What if Harvey took the work of two classes at once? He could then catch up faster with his normal level and begin to work on that bright future all the sooner. They talked for over an hour. Harvey sat spellbound. At the end of the conversation he told Couch that he had faith in him. And he told him something that Couch would remember for the rest of his life: "Men like you have built empires." By the end of that afternoon, Couch not only agreed to Neff's proposition, he left for home charged with a purpose and ambition for his life that never left him. It was the character of him and Neff that made the traditional words of encouragement between pupil and teacher come alive with meaning and set the cadence for the remainder of Couch's life. Pat Neff would leave that class and go on to become governor of Texas and later president of Baylor University. Harvey Couch would leave believing he could build an empire.

Harvey worked with Pat Neff for almost two years before he was forced to leave to help support his three brothers and two sisters. Harvey, of course, wanted to go to work for the railroad. But so did a lot of other people. All he could do was put in his application and wait. In the meantime he found a position as a drugstore clerk in Magnolia.

Dr. H.A. Longino, a partner in the store, took a special interest in the nineteen-year-old. He was especially pleased by Harvey's sincere manner. In a community of straightforward townspeople, Harvey's slow-talking style was appreciated. Couch proved to be a hard worker and his honesty was exceptional. One day Longino found that Harvey had left an IOU in the cash drawer for some stamps he had borrowed. Longino was greatly impressed. "It would do well to trust a boy who would charge himself for stamps," he told his partner. They gave Harvey the added responsibility of collecting overdue accounts.

To be sure, Harvey Couch did not consider himself a slick talker. Only in the last two years had he met new people on a regular basis. His duties at the drugstore were mainly solitary labors such as pasting labels on medicine bottles. Now he was expected to talk people out of their money. As he left for the first day on his collection route, Harvey thought real hard about how much he needed this job.

His first collection was nearly nine miles outside of town. He rented a bicycle and began to pedal toward the farm. As he puffed down the dusty road he tried to decide whether he was sweating from the heat or the tension he felt inside. Finally he arrived at the farm. He leaned his bike against the split rail fence and tried to gather his thoughts, wiping the sweat from his brow. "How am I going to do this?" he wondered. No answer came. He took a deep breath and headed for the front porch. A grizzled farmer stood on the other side of the screen door.

"Hello. I'm Harvey Couch," he said as he approached.

"I was wonderin' if you was goin' to stand out there all day," the old farmer responded.

Harvey turned red. He stood on the porch and examined the dust on the tops of his shoes. There was a silence.

"Can I he'p ya?" the farmer inquired.

"Um, I hope so," Harvey managed.

"What is it?" The farmer opened the screen door and came out on to the porch.

"Can we sit down?" Harvey asked.

"Well, sure. Sit yorese'f down right there," he said, pointing at two wooden rocking chairs. They went to the chairs and sat down. The farmer offered his pouch of tobacco. "Want some?"

"Thanks."

They sat for a moment quietly arranging the tobacco in their mouths. Harvey did not chew tobacco but he knew enough not to swallow. Finally, Harvey broke the silence.

"I work for Dr. Longino. I'm his new assistant."

The old man turned and stared carefully at Harvey. He then began to rock slowly back and forth.

"A man can't pay if he don't have the money," he said, seemingly to himself.

"No one can argue with that," Harvey answered.

They continued to rock in silence.

"I'd pay if I had the money."

"Of course you would," Harvey responded. "You're an honest man."

"I sure am," the man said sharply.

As they continued to rock, Harvey looked out at the farm. It looked a lot like his family's old farm. He began to talk about the farm and his mother and father. They talked for quite a while. Finally Harvey got up to leave.

"I sure wish I could he'p you," the farmer said as Harvey was climbing on his bicycle.

"I know you'd pay if you had the money." As he glanced toward the barn a thought occurred to Harvey. "Say, what if I could convince Dr. Longino to take the spare corn that you have in your crib in the barn in payment? Then we could clear up this debt."

The old farmer nearly swallowed his tobacco. "What?" he coughed.

"Well, I'm not sure it would work. But I can see all that corn stored in your barn—I'm sure you'd have enough extra to pay your bill in corn. I don't know if Dr. Longino would agree to it, but I'm sure willing to try if you are!" Harvey threw out his hand.

"Sure," the farmer croaked. He weakly offered his hand.

"This may work," Harvey said, pumping the hand of the farmer. He then picked up his bike and was off. The old farmer watched Harvey ride off in a cloud of dust and wondered whether he had been slickered. He decided that he had not.

When the news came that his application for a job on the St. Louis Railroad had finally been accepted, Harvey viewed it with mixed emotions. Working on a railroad had been his goal since he first saw a locomotive, but during his months at the drugstore he and Longino had become close friends. Longino treated him like a son and Harvey appreciated his kindness. Longino had raised Couch's salary to $240 a year; the railroad, however, paid three times as much as Longino could afford, and Harvey had a family of brothers and sisters to support. This had to be his main consideration. After all these years, Harvey was finally going to work on a train. "This won't be work," he thought.

Harvey Crowley Couch around the turn of the century

Chapter Two

THE IDEA OF WORKING on a railroad had been a dream of Couch's for a long time. He had labored for months on a correspondence course in an effort to pass the test to become a railway mail clerk. He originally had designs on an engineer spot but relinquished that dream due to his parents' concern for his safety. In March 1898, 21-year-old Couch bid Longino farewell and headed for St. Louis to report for duty.

On the train to St. Louis, Couch met O.W. Clark, a young man who was also reporting for his first day on the railroad. Clark wanted eventually to become a medical doctor. The two fell in together and became fast friends, promising to support each other in their new jobs in the big city.

Upon arrival, Couch and Clark were assigned for duty on the small mail car for duty for the run from St. Louis to Texarkana, Texas. Couch's indoctrination into the real world of railroading was anything but a dream. The young man began to sort what seemed like a sea of letters in the car as wave after wave of more mail was delivered by incoming trains to the St. Louis station. The train finally left St. Louis at 3:25 a.m. They worked all night and through the next day as the train stopped at each town along its route to pick up more and more mail. Except for breaks to wolf down the food they carried in their paper sacks, it was a continuous effort. Finally, at 8:50 that evening, they arrived in Texarkana. The train had stopped but it seemed as if it were still moving; their heads were swimming. As they stepped on the station platform, the wooden deck rolled under their feet. Couch and Clark looked at each other, their eyes swollen with fatigue. Couch grabbed the chief clerk, who was leaving the platform.

"How do I resign from this job?"

"You can't resign. You signed on for three years. The only way you can get out of this job is to die."

The clerk turned on his heel and headed off toward the terminal hotel. Couch and Clark looked at each other again. Money for a hotel was not in their budget. Reluctantly, they climbed back on the mail car. They grabbed mail sacks, piled them on the floor, collapsed on top, and were quickly asleep.

They awoke with a start as the train started to move. The head clerk was back on the car.

"What's going on?" they demanded.

"We're heading back," the clerk answered. "Come on now, get to work."

Couch grabbed at his watch. He couldn't believe his eyes. They had been asleep nineteen hours.

For a year, Couch was substitute clerk or "helper" on the St. Louis–Texarkana run, leaving St. Louis every four days. He was then transferred as head clerk to the Memphis–Texarkana run.

The country was still trying to recover from a depression of the 1890s. Many young men Couch's age were heading north to work in the industrialized cities. Opportunities in the South, outside of farming, were limited. Harvey Couch was lucky. He was secure in what everyone considered a "good" job. He was sending money home to his family with each paycheck. But Couch was not content. The influence of Pat Neff remained. He told Clark that he was determined to "go somewhere, get somewhere, be something." He knew that his somewhere was not to be found on this rail line.

The Memphis–Texarkana run was less demanding than his previous route. He found he had time to visit with merchants along the route. Harvey's experience with eggs helped him see the need to market surplus eggs. He worked out an arrangement with stores and farmers to distribute their excess eggs through his contacts in Memphis. He made one cent on each carton; it

Harvey Couch (left) sorting mail for St. Louis Railroad

wasn't much money, but it was extra money. And it was teaching him that perhaps he could create his opportunities rather than wait for them.

Clark was transferred to his car. Harvey sometimes worked double duty so that his friend could take occassional medical classes. Couch knew what it was like to have a dream.

Joel, Arkansas, was a water stop for the train. As they pulled in one day, Couch saw a construction gang raising a pole along the line.

"Moving the telegraph line?" Couch asked.

"Nope," the construction boss shouted as the train rolled past, "we're puttin' up a long-distance telephone wire."

Alexander Graham Bell had received his patent for the telephone on March 7, 1876. The development of telephone service since that time had been slow due to the lack of investors willing to gamble on what seemed to be a speculative project. Western Union, which had the communication monopoly in the country at that time, did everything in its power to stop it. The major obstacle to its development, however, was its novelty. Since the dawn of time, people thought, homes had been run without a telephone in each house, and things had worked out pretty well. Why spend money for one now? The country's telegraph system was at its peak. It was quick, efficient and cheap. For pennies you could send a telegram across the nation and your message would be received within hours.

Telephone service, in contrast, was questionable. Primitive equipment and static made friends sound like strangers. Privacy was suddenly banished from daily life. A home with a telephone seemed to welcome intrusions any time of the day or night. Mark Twain cracked, "If Bell had invented a muffler or a gag, he would have done a real service." But there was something very compelling about sending your voice through those wires to a friend who could also talk back to you. Almost as if foreseeing the telephone's eventual triumph, Twain installed one of the first telephones in his own home.

The first two decades of the development of the telephone were slow. The technical problems of the new service ate up capital at a furious rate. Development was limited to areas that could produce the most revenue for the least expenditure—the big cities. During this time Bell's company held the monopoly on the patents that made phone service possible, but by 1893 and 1894 these grants were running out and the courts were refusing to enforce Bell's claims to sole ownership. The country's major metropolitan areas had already signed on with the Bell system, but this left countless smaller towns without service and receptive to any offers that would bring them the telephone. Competitors with ambition and copper wire were springing up overnight. Bell and the newborn telephone competitors were now in a race to win franchises to provide service to small towns across America.

Over the next few days Couch followed the workers' progress and badgered them with questions. Telephones seemed amazingly simple—just wires and poles and a few phone sets. Couch realized that this was the opportunity he had been waiting for, but could he make it happen? He wanted to keep his job on the train while trying out his new venture, so he needed a new route that would take him somewhere where there was no phone service yet, someplace like home...It would be years before the Bell Company would make it to the area around Magnolia in southwest Arkansas.

Couch decided he needed the route that ran from near Magnolia south into Louisiana. He paid another clerk $50 to exchange routes with him. Pete Couch, Harvey's brother, was now old enough to enlist into his business. Pete would meet him at a stopover near their home and bring Harvey's lunch. He would climb into the mail car and listen intently as Harvey discussed options for starting a telephone company.

Couch needed capital to make his new enterprise work. After paying the other clerk to exchange routes, he had exactly $156 saved from his railway wages. He was still sending much of his salary home, so the prospect of acquiring start-up capital on his own seemed bleak.

Undaunted, Couch approached Ben Cheen, the postmaster in Bienville, Louisiana, and told him his plans. He asked Cheen to become his partner.

"I haven't got any money, Harvey," Cheen protested.

"Neither have I," Harvey smiled. "That's why I think we'd made good partners!"

Cheen could not argue with this logic. They became partners. Thus the North Louisiana Telephone Company was started.

Couch's personality was now becoming an important factor in his activities. People liked him. They wanted him to do well. Couch was developing the ability to make others believe in his dreams. He asked a local merchant to let him borrow enough copper line for his proposed company, to be paid back when his phone system became operational in the spring. He said he had "perfect faith" that his system would work. The merchant believed him and let him borrow the wire.

Couch's next task was to raise money to pay the workers he would need to string the line. He did this by selling coupon books entitling the buyer to $5.50 worth of telephone service for $5.00. This was a tremendous challenge. Five dollars was a lot of money. In a poor farming community, a family could live on that kind of money for a week. During the two hours' layover in Bienville, Couch would hit the streets telling anyone who would listen about the wonders of the modern telephone. Selling an intangible product such as telephone service to people who had never seen a telephone, for a telephone company that was not yet in existence, might be nearly impossible.

But not for Harvey Couch. He was the exception because people wanted him to succeed, not in a vague, general sort of way, but strongly, as they would want their son or best friend to succeed. He could talk about the grandest schemes with simple words that people could understand and believe, his dreams, in a sense, then becoming their own. In a short time Couch had sold enough booklets to pay for construction of the line upon its completion. It was the realization of a dream that everyone had bought into for only five dollars.

At first construction was awkward. It took some time for Harvey, Pete, and the crew to learn the fundamentals of line construction. The logistics of moving creosote-covered poles by wagon across farms were tremendous. Mules were used to raise the poles. Slowly, the Couches and crew learned procedures to speed the process.

The line was stretched from the postmaster's office in Bienville to the postmaster's office in McNeil. The phone system was cumbersome yet simple. A caller from Bienville to McNeil would first approach Ben Cheen at the post office and say he wanted to make a call. Ben would cross over to the wall model phone and turn the crank several times, causing the phone set to ring on the wall at the McNeil post office. The McNeil postmaster would answer the phone, Ben would tell him who the call was for, and he would then send a messenger to fetch the called party to the line. During the delay the caller would loiter patiently by the phone. When the called party arrived he would then turn the phone crank at McNeil, causing the Bienville phone to ring. Ben Cheen would answer the phone and hand it to the caller while collecting 25 cents' worth of payment coupons.

The first day of the service Couch decided to turn into a celebration. He knew that in other towns, first-time callers were sometimes afflicted with a kind of stage fright. He could not afford to let people get used to the new phone system slowly; he had to get them using the phone at once. The first callers were the mayors of both towns. Everyone crowded around the telephones and listened anxiously to half of the historic conversation. At the end of the conversation, everyone applauded and clamored to be the next to use the new device. Most found they didn't have much to say after the first "hellos," but Couch smiled as almost everyone promised to call back "real soon." Service was free that day to encourage everyone to learn the new telephone process.

Because of the messenger dependency of the new system, the phone's most important customers were business people who worked in the city. Although the telegraph system was better developed and even quicker for one-way messages, the telephone was better suited for more complex messages and for haggling over the price of goods or services. Over the next few months Couch's North Louisiana Telephone Company was used consistently by both local business and the farm community.

The next step was obvious to Couch. He and Cheen needed to expand into other communities along the route and perhaps add a switchboard to enable calls to be placed directly into homes in their new company's service area. Ben Cheen did not think this was obvious at all. Things were fine the way they were, he said. They were receiving a nice return on their investment; there was no reason to risk any more capital. Couch didn't want to play it safe. He wanted to build an empire. The two men couldn't find a compromise.

Finally Cheen said, "Look, Harvey, either I buy you out or you buy me out."

Couch agreed to buy Cheen's share of the company for

$1,500. Cheen gave him the weekend to come up with the money, or Cheen would buy the company from Couch.

Couch didn't have the money. Friday night, alone in his hotel room, he debated the possibilities. There was only one available to him. Saturday morning he boarded the train back home to Magnolia to see his old friend, Dr. Longino.

Longino was pleased to see his young friend again. Harvey, now 27, was beginning to fill out some, but Longino found he hadn't changed. Quickly, Harvey launched into a description of his experiences with his phone company. He told Longino of Cheen's ultimatum and then blurted out his request: Would Longino become partners with him in the new telephone venture?

Longino did not know much about telephones, but he knew Harvey. Couch was like a son to the 46-year-old Longino, and, much like everyone else, he wanted the young man to succeed. He had one question: "How much do you need?"

On the train back to Bienville, Harvey was excited and now more determined than ever. Cheen had invested little beyond his time in the new venture. Longino had provided what seemed to Couch a fortune. The year was 1904. It was the beginning of a new century and the start of an empire that Harvey was positive he could create. He felt he couldn't ask for a better start. He could now buy Cheen's part of the business for $1,000, which Longino would then buy for $1,500. Couch would put an additional $500 of his own money in the business to match Longino's investment. To top it all off, Longino lent him $1,500 more to cover expenses. Couch was now head of a corporation with a paid capitalization of $5,000. Also, the corporation's ranks were beginning to swell. J.L. Longino, Dr. Longino's 25-year-old nephew, would be coming aboard to assist in the expanded operations. Longino had recently graduated from the University of Arkansas with a degree in electrical engineering. If the company was going to expand according to Couch's vision it needed this type of technical expertise.

Almost immediately, Couch puts his plans for expansion into effect. He kept his job on the railroad so that he could funnel more of the money that the company made back into it for expansion and equipment. Soon his crew, working under Pete's direction, following the route set out by J.L., was working full time stringing lines into the nearby towns of Gibsland and Arcadia. He was also beginning to establish switchboards in each town so that calls could be made through the switchboards between any two homes in the North Louisiana Telephone Company's system. Couch took equal pride in his company's growth and its service to farmers isolated over hundreds of miles. He was beginning to believe that this was the best purpose of any business—to help develop and serve the community in which it was located.

Growth continued at a feverish pace, including negotiations to bring his phone system to Athens, Louisiana. While working on the Athens project, Couch met and fell in love with Jessie Johnson. He quickly proposed, and they were married by a Methodist minister in the Johnsons' living room on October 4, 1904. There was time for only a brief honeymoon, since Jessie was indispensible as the newest employee of the North Louisiana Telephone Company. She took over the accounting of the Gibsland exchange.

By the next year, 1905, Couch knew that he could no longer remain an employee of the railroad. Telephone-hungry communities were now demanding that Couch and his associates bring the new phone system to them. Couch joined the venture full-time to help meet the demand. He knew they were in a race.

The Southwestern Bell Company was becoming well aware of the activities of companies like Couch's. They were no longer treating these rivals as nuisances but now as actual threats to the survival of the Bell system. They were increasing their expansion activities in an effort to contain this new danger.

Couch and company could figuratively, if not literally, feel the ever-tightening encirclement of the Bell wires. Workdays seemed endless as the North Louisiana system sped to complete lines from Arkansas and Louisiana into Texas and Oklahoma. Most of the extended lines paralleled the railroads' right of way. Couch found that a few well-placed cigars among his old railway buddies would allow him to place telephone poles on empty train cars. One of Couch's crew would ride with the poles and boot them out, one at a time, along the route. Pete and his work gang would follow along behind setting up each pole as they came to it. The pressure to connect towns before the Bell Company arrived was tremendous. On one occasion a desperate Pete "borrowed" a train to distribute poles for a new line. Fortunately, he returned it before it was discovered missing.

By 1910, North Louisiana and Southwestern Bell were competing head to head for each town. The few towns that remained to be connected with telephone service became even more vital to each company. The Bell system had tremendous resources, but the North Louisiana Company continued to do well. It was a local company with many satisfied customers. Even more importantly, Couch continued to be able to win people to his dream.

When he won the franchise for Fordyce, Arkansas, Couch saw the opportunity to construct a long-distance line to Little Rock for the benefit of his entire system. The Bell Company also saw Couch's opportunity. According to state law whatever company connected long-distance service first would have exclusive rights to that service. The Bell system planned to use their greater resources to construct a Little Rock–Fordyce line before Couch could react. Almost as if playing a game of chess, Harvey anticipated Bell's move. Working day and night, Pete and his crew put up a line from Fordyce to Little Rock in six days, while Bell was still marshaling its forces.

But by 1911, the game was over. The North Louisiana Telephone Company had constructed more than 1,500 miles of line servicing 50 exchanges in four states. However, the Bell system now completely surrounded Couch. He could easily maintain the system he had created, but maintaining something had no charms for him. He wanted to build, to keep on growing. Reluctantly, he agreed to sell to the Bell system. After several months of negotiation, the two companies agreed to a price of well over $1 million. Dr. Longino's return on his $5,000 investment was over $70,000. After other investors were paid off, Couch's share still amounted to over $1 million.

If Pat Neff had not sat down with Harvey seventeen years before, Couch might have been tempted to take his share of the money, buy a farm near his home, and live comfortably for the rest of his life. But the drive to build, to create, was strong in him, and he was discovering that he could create opportunities—opportunities that people mistakenly thought were nonexistent in Arkansas. Certainly, there was a lack of capital in the area, but Couch felt the main root of underdevelopment was apathy.

People didn't believe "empires" were possible, so as a result they never came to be.

Couch, on the other hand, claimed "perfect faith" in what was possible. If he could, Couch wanted to be an example to Arkansas of what was possible, as Pat Neff had been an example to him. Although the telephone business was now dominated by the Bell Companies, Couch felt that other opportunities were limitless in the Southwest. He wanted to build another company that would provide the kind of personal satisfaction his telephone company had. He wanted another business that could be an extension of his faith, could help build Arkansas, and most importantly, could be of service to people. He searched for something to fill those qualifications, but the only work experience he had involved stringing copper wires on creosote-covered poles. He hoped to find a new line of work that would utilize the knowledge he had already acquired.

Chapter Three

IN MANY WAYS the development of electric power in the United States paralleled that of telephone service. Both utilities were developed at an exceedingly slow pace due to the tremendous capital investments required and the problems inherent in any new technology. Electric growth did not have to overcome faulty transmissions but it did require knowledgeable handling. Ironically, electric development was also hampered considerably by the creator of the first practical incandescent bulb—Thomas Edison.

Edison's early electric experiments were conducted using direct current (DC) power. The first generating station in America was Edison's Pearl Street Station in New York City. Built in 1882, the station used DC power to light the surrounding homes and businesses of the neighborhood. The problem with DC power generation was the number of generating stations it required to service an entire city. The cost of development of several stations in each city effectively prevented electric development.

However, by the next year, 1883, successful demonstrations of alternating current (AC) power were conducted in Europe. The advantage of AC power was that it could be "stepped up" or increased for transmission and then "stepped down" or decreased by transformers for distribution to individual homes and businesses. This would allow a single generating station to supply an entire city.

The economic and practical advantages of AC power were obvious, but Edison was vocally against it. He claimed the dangers of AC power were too great to ignore. He publicly challenged AC advocates to a "duel" of electricity. He would hook himself and any challenger to the two forms of electric power: Edison to DC and the challenger to AC. The voltage of each would be slowly increased. The survivor of the duel would then be declared the winner. Because AC power is deadly at a much lower voltage than DC, Edison had no takers to his challenge.

Since most people considered Edison to be the man who invented electricity itself, the weight of his opposition was almost overwhelming. Investors waited for Edison to perfect a direct current transmission system, but Edison seemed unable to overcome the many difficulties in distributing DC power without the necessary DC transformer.

The Westinghouse Company, however, saw this as an opportunity to take the new electric service market away from Edison by developing the more effective AC system for general use.

Edison was a formidable opponent. Besides the respect he commanded in the general population, he knew how to use publicity for his own advantage. To illustrate how unsafe AC power was he developed the first electric chair, which used, of course, AC current. He also began to refer to the early victims of electrocution as being "westinghoused."

In 1896, the first heavy power installation was completed by the Westinghouse Company. It was a hydroelectric generating station on Niagara Falls that could generate as much as 15,000 horsepower, as compared to 900 at Edison's Pearl Street Station. With this practical demonstration of the effectiveness of AC power the confusion over the future of electric development was resolved. Although there continued to be proponents of DC power, Edison included, the investment money now fell into line behind the development of AC power.

To be sure, the path to electric development was not smooth. In Arkansas, electric development was erratic. In 1893 Little Rock was first lit by arc lamps, predecessors of incandescent lights that used direct current. Arc lamps were so intense they could light an entire city street and as such were unsuitable for home use. Their first use was in public places such as hotels or stores where large areas could be lit.

In the years that followed, as incandescent lights became available, company after company sprang up and failed. The equipment was expensive to maintain and could not provide effective widespread service. As newer technology became available, companies across the state found they did not have the resources to keep up.

The *Chicago Tribune* reported on August 17, 1912, that the "whole town" of Russellville, Arkansas, was boycotting their local utility company, Russellville Water and Light Company. They were in arms because of the poor service they believed it was providing. Among the boycotters' demands was a reduction of rates from 20 to 15 cents per kilowatt-hour.

Throughout the first part of the twentieth century in towns all over Arkansas, electric companies were started, only to fail soon afterward. In 1900 it was advertised that "someone" had counted "over 200" potential uses for electricity on the farm. But by 1911, how electricity could be brought to farms in Arkansas was a problem yet to be solved.

In the two years since 1911, when Couch had sold his telephone company, he had begun to study the tremendous difficulties in bringing electricity to Arkansas. The major obstacle was, as always, the lack of investment capital in the state. The dozens of electric companies that had sprung up throughout the state were hamstrung by a shortage of appropriate start-up capital. The new electric generating equipment was expensive. There was a lengthy delay in pay-back on the equipment, as many customers waited to see how secure the new companies were before signing on. Equipment was subject to frequent breakdowns, which always seemed to occur at night. Electric companies were forced to raise their rates continually in an effort to stay afloat, thus angering the customers they did have.

The capital available to make an expensive operation like an electric utility work was invested in the big northern cities where pay-back was more immediate and line distribution easier. In Arkansas, where there were dozens of scattered communities, intermixed with isolated farms, the prospects of quick return on an investment were dismal. As had happened with telephone service during its early years, electric utility companies would experience delays in making their way to farm states like Arkansas.

Couch saw opportunity in the current situation, but he was also well aware of the dangers. Electric service was much more complex and expensive than telephone service. Couch was now a wealthy man, but his personal wealth was no match for the amount of investment necessary to create a electric utility company of the type he imagined.

He proposed to eliminate the chronic equipment problems by establishing an interconnected electric system much like the telephone systems he had created. The advantage of an interconnected electric system was that one community could be powered by any one of several different power sources. This, he hoped, would eliminate the outages created by broken equipment and build a more satisfied customer base. The concept was simple but it was unique in the Southwest. The problem with this type of system was that, at first, it would be more expensive than creating separate power systems for each town, since transmission lines would have to be constructed between cities served by Couch. As the system was developed Couch hoped that several small communities could be served by a central distribution point, thereby saving money over a period of time. He now needed to find an area where he could try his interconnected utility concept with the lowest start-up cost possible.

At the beginning of this century there was only about 80,000 in primary horsepower being generated in the state. Outside of New Orleans, no industry in Arkansas, Louisiana, or Mississippi used electric power. The limited number of industries in Arkansas depended on self-created energy. This energy was steam. Steam boilers could drive turbines and belts and power a wide range of functions. One of the biggest users of this steam energy in Arkansas was the lumber industry. Arkansas was still covered by hundreds of miles of forests, and lumber from Arkansas was being cut to build much of the rest of the country.

Once again, Couch wanted to start his new company in the area around his home in the southern part of the state. Malvern and Arkadelphia had already awarded franchises for electric service to two different companies, which had both failed. They were soliciting bids for a company to assume the duties of the failed companies. This seemed a likely spot for Couch to try his idea of interconnected electric service, since the operating equipment left by the defunct companies was not adequate.

At first Couch considered building a small hydroelectric dam on the Ouachita River. He, Longino, and a work crew, guided by Flave Carpenter, an ex–riverboat captain, climbed the hills on either side of the Ouachita charting probable spots for a dam. At one point during what seemed like the endless charting up and down the hills, one of the workers shopped short and sat down exhausted.

"Say, Mr. Couch," he said, "don't you ever stop and just have fun?"

"Isn't this fun?" Couch replied, mystified.

Couch and Longino presented their findings to Dean W.M. Gladson, Professor of Engineering at the University of Arkansas. Gladson carefully studied the charts and plans of what Couch was now calling the Arkansas Power Company. Gladson agreed that two or possibly three hydroelectric dams were possible from an engineering standpoint, but that from a business view he recommended against it. There was no demand as yet for the amount of power this dam would create. Couch and Longino agreed that they should wait until demand increased, but this left him with the problem of supplying Arkadelphia and Malvern with electricity.

The Arkansas Land and Lumber Company was working at Malvern, using steam boilers to power their sawing and milling projects. Couch heard about their operations while searching for someone to team with him in the cogeneration of electric power. In October 1913, Couch went to inspect the Arkansas Land and Lumber property. He was amazed that sawdust, a great source of fuel for steam boilers, was being treated as a waste product. Also, he noticed that Arkansas Land and Lumber was preparing to construct a new boiler on the property. Couch saw this as an opportunity to buy steam from their boiler system to power a 550-kilowatt turbine.

Couch contacted H.H. Foster, the president of Arkansas Land and Lumber, and arranged for a meeting. Couch explained his concept of power cogeneration using sawdust for fuel and tapping in to Foster's new boiler. Foster was at once intrigued by the idea. He agreed that the new boiler could run exclusively on what the lumbermen called "hogdust." But he was leery of letting another company on his property to build poles and construct lines. Besides, both Malvern and Arkadelphia had already had bad experiences with electric power companies, and he knew of Couch by reputation only. He didn't want his company to be associated with what might turn out to be another fly-by-night electric company.

Over the next few days, Couch brought his persuasiveness to bear on Foster through repeated phone calls and personal visits. By the end of the month Foster was won over. The lumberman was convinced as much by Couch's sunny personality as by the economic sense of the proposal.

On December 2, 1913, the contract between the Arkansas Power Company and the Arkansas Land and Lumber Company was signed. For $300 a month Couch would buy steam from the lumber company's boilers to give Malvern and Arkadelphia 24-hour electric service for the first time. After Couch left, Foster realized that in the whirlwind of Couch's sales campaign he had failed to include one of his major stockholders in the details of the new deal.

Immediately, he sat down to write this stockholder in Wisconsin. After gingerly introducing the subject, he wrote:

> The only thing that I feel that it is necessary to say by way of explanation is in regard to the fact that we have not referred the matter to the northern stockholders before we finally closed it up...Three or four hundred dollars per month may not seem very attractive in and of itself, but if this plant we are creating has a life of fifteen years, please compute what it means in the life of the plant that would not otherwise be available to us and the entire revenue represented by the contract the result of our refuse. I hope this contract will please you...

After leaving Foster, Couch went to the Malvern railroad station where he would catch a train back to his temporary headquaters in the State National Bank Building in Little Rock. As he waited, he began figuring up the projected costs of the new plan. He was hoping to be on line by the middle of 1914, but many things remained to be done, and after boarding the train he began to list them all on the back of an envelope. He would start by moving his rapidly growing family to Arkadelphia. They were ready for a bigger house since they were quickly outgrowing their home in Little Rock. Tom Couch had died in 1908, and Manie had moved in with the family to help manage the growing brood of children. Harvey and Jessie now had three sons— Johnson Olin, born in 1905; Harvey Jr., born in 1908; and Kirke, born in 1912—and were planning on more children. The idea of the move pleased Harvey, as he preferred for the virtues of small-town living to influence his children rather than those of Little Rock.

He also needed to call a board meeting of his Arkansas Power Company to discuss the final details of the Arkansas Land and Lumber Company arrangement. Arkansas Power had only recently been incorporated with an optimistic capital stock of $500,000 authorized. The articles of incorporation stated that the "place of business is to be located at Arkadelphia, Malvern and other points in the State of Arkansas." The final notation for the back of the envelope was the estimate of construction costs for a transmission line to tie Malvern to Arkadelphia. Basing his estimate on his years in the telephone business, Couch began to figure in his head the costs for material and labor. He estimated the construction line to be somewhere around 22 miles. He then wrote his estimation of the final cost of the project at the bottom of the envelope. With all this done, he sat back and enjoyed being on a train once again.

At the meeting of Arkansas Power's board of directors on January 28, 1914, Couch discussed the particulars of the new generating plant and plans for the future. He would build a brick building ten feet in front of the lumber company boiler room and then install two 550-kilowatt generators. Over the 22 miles to Arkadelphia, he would construct a 22,000-volt, three-phase line that would parallel the Missouri Pacific Railroad line. In order not to delay construction, J.L. Longino had charted the entire length of the route on foot. Construction was to begin immediately.

Couch also got approval from his board to purchase the Magnolia and Camden plants that were up for sale. This, however, introduced a problem that lay at the heart of Couch's dream of an interconnected system for the state. Arkansas banks were refusing to lend money in amounts necessary for such a system. The banks, after seeing scores of electric companies default on loans and go quickly under, did not want to finance an even more extensive, expensive project. Some had even said they were content to wait the ten years or so it would take the northern utilities to make their way south to Arkansas. Couch could not accept this. How could anyone who had the power to change things accept ten years of inadequate city water due to a lack of electric pumping stations, or ten years without the heavy industry that could provide jobs to thousands of Arkansans, or ten years of the bucket brigade when it could be replaced by modern fire protection? Farmers were still living in the nineteenth century with their kerosene lamps and mule power. Couch felt that these bankers' purpose should be not only to make a profit but to help build Arkansas. The bankers, however, felt their main obligation was to their stockholders.

Couch told his board that he wanted to go over the heads of the Arkansas banks to New York City, where most investment capital originated. Charles McCain, the head of the Banker's Trust in Little Rock, had written a letter of introduction for Couch to an investment banker McCain knew in New York. Couch wanted to use this New York connection to begin to court investment capital and finance the system outside of the state. In 1914, going to New York in search of investors seemed as likely as going to the moon, but Couch won the board to his plan. It was their only hope. If the Arkansas Power Company was to grow, it would need the amounts of money that only New York City banks were willing to provide.

Couch left almost immediately for New York. Using the entree McCain had given him, he went directly to the offices of the Guaranty Trust Company, walked into the lobby...and lost his nerve. He had never seen an office building so grand. It seemed to be almost made of gold. Every day for a week he walked from his hotel to the bank and then became overwhelmed by the thought of selling a New York banker on the prospects of an Arkansas electric company. By the end of the week his money had run out. He realized that he must at least try to sell the banker. So he rode the elevator up to the executive offices and presented his letter of introduction to John Watkins. He launched into a detailed description of his new power company, his plans, and the wonders of the state of Arkansas. Watkins listened intently as Couch related his story. He decided he liked Couch and would help him in any way he could. When Couch was finished with his presentation Watkins, like Longino over a decade before, had one question:

"How much money do you need?"

That afternoon as Harvey walked down the streets of New York toward his hotel, his feet did not touch the pavement. Watkins had agreed to foot an initial loan of $200,000. Couch was amazed that this much money was readily available, but most of all, he was amazed that New York bankers were just as human as anyone else. He would be coming back to New York, he decided.

During the remainder of 1914, Couch oversaw the construction of the Malvern–Arkadelphia line and the planning for future growth of the Arkansas Power Company. Although he realized that cogeneration with lumber companies was not an effective long-term possibility, he wanted to purchase franchises in timber country to tie in with these fuel sources as much as possible. Joint projects benefited the young company both directly and indirectly. Since Couch and his men were still learning the electric business, they did not always hit upon the most efficient practices at once. For example, an engineering study of a proposed APC system in Stamps indicated there would be as much as a 25 percent loss of power being distributed through the system. Such losses could be avoided when Couch tied in to a system with better transmission; then the result was usually savings that could not be ignored.

On September 8, additional investors were found within the state, and Arkansas Power was reorganized as Arkansas Light and Power. It continued to do business as Arkansas Power in Malvern and Arkadelphia.

By December 1914 the line was completed and the generators were in place at Arkansas Land and Lumber. Service could begin immediately, but Couch took a few days to plan for the opening of the first interconnected electric service in the state. He wanted to outdo any of the publicity campaigns he had used for his telephone service. He could waste no time in developing his service; it had been a full year of investment with no return since he first acquired franchises for the two cities. He wanted ceremonies that would make the paper—something appropriate for the occasion.

The Malvern power plant, which Couch acquired in 1914

On December 18, 1914, the front page of the *Arkansas Gazette* was filled with the horrors of the World War, but on page two, Harvey Couch and the Arkansas Power Company were featured. The article, headlined "Two Cities Enjoy New Light System," went on to say:

> The opening of the new white way [those streets now lit by electricity] and the advent of a new electrical epoch in this city were celebrated tonight in a manner like unto the pomp of Roman triumph—Society, with its beauty and culture, and business interests with their practical expositions, co-operated in making the pageant and carnival the greatest thing of its kind ever seen in this city.

Those who were lucky enough to be there on December 17 to see "the pomp of the Roman triumph" started the day in Malvern. Couch had arranged for a special train car to bring him and the board of directors. It pulled into Malvern shortly after noon. A delegation from the city, including the mayor and the newly crowned "Queens of Electricity" for Malvern and Arkadelphia, met them at the station. From the station a parade led by the local high school band traveled through the streets of the city and out to the power plant. At the plant H.H. Foster beamed as his little daughter, Dorothy May, was given the honor of pushing the button which started the huge steam generators. Then the crowd watched as the two queens turned the switches that sent electric current to their home towns. The crowd exploded with applause and cheering. Then, with bands playing patriotic marches, Couch led the crowd to the Bryan building in Malvern.

At the Bryan building the mayors of Little Rock, Hope, Malvern, and Arkadelphia gave speeches. Harvey then took the podium and promised the faithful electric service he believed would give Malvern all the advantages the twentieth century could provide. As the ceremonies ended, Couch gathered the group of mayors and the two Electric Queens and boarded the train for Arkadelphia.

At Arkadelphia, Couch and the dignitaries were met by the Arkadelphia City Council. They climbed on open carriages and followed the Cadet Corps of Ouachita College through the streets of Arkadelphia. They arrived at the so-called white way and Florence Beck, the queen representing Arkadelphia, wearing a crown made of light bulbs, turned a switch that flooded the streets with electric lights. The crowd applauded loudly, gathering near the street lights as the sky grew dark on the mild winter night.

Couch then led the crowd to the carnival auditorium at Sixth and Clinton Streets as the band played to escort the crowd. At the auditorium the queen's court was introduced, soloists sang, and the mayors repeated their speeches with appropriate changes for the new city. The evening lasted quite late. After the ceremony, citizens could tour booths set up by the Women's Library Association, the Campfire Girls, and other civic groups. There was also a display of the new electric appliances. Harvey was hoarse and his hand was sore after talking and shaking hands so long, but he insisted on staying until he had talked to everyone present. Though he was excited by the accomplishment of Arkansas Light and Power, he was proudest when his secretary presented him with his original estimate of line costs that he had made on the back of an envelope. He had been correct to within twelve dollars. As the townspeople left the auditorium and walked down the lighted streets, they would stop and gaze up now and then at the bright streetlights which they thought symbolized nothing less than the future of Arkadelphia.

Chapter Four

ALMOST IMMEDIATELY, Couch began expanding the service area of the newly renamed Arkansas Light and Power Company. He included the homes along the 22-mile route from Malvern to Arkadelphia. To each small community he brought a reliability of service thought impossible only a year previously. He also added in quick succession isolated municipal generating stations that he planned to unite one day in a single transmission system. Couch was using capital from New York to add Newport on June 5, Paragould on July 1, and Morrilton on October 14, 1915.

The next year, 1916, Couch continued his rapid expansion and developed the company's second central generating station in Russellville, which would serve that city along with Plumerville, Dardanelle, Morrilton, and Atkins with an 83,000-volt transmission line. The plant was built by a coal field so that a steady supply of fuel was guaranteed. Couch would also supply coal for stoves to homes in the area.

Coal was not the only product AL&P was supplying. In many communities, Couch was forced to purchase the entire range of public services from the local company. Often he would acquire the town's electric, gas, and water systems. Local ice services, important in pre-electric days, usually remained part of the spectrum of utilities even after the demand for ice waned, and Couch would buy them as well. Later, in Pine Bluff, he would

Linemen at work, early 1920s

*Harrison linemen around 1924: (left to right) V.M. Kellogg,
Lucerne Covington, Frank Marlin, and Howard Stark*

also acquire the streetcar system.

With this first shaping of an interconnected power system, Couch found that he was facing what would continue for many years—peak load demands. Peak load is the maximum demand placed on an electric system during any period of time. Peak load required that the company be able to provide electric service at high levels, if only for short periods of time. Couch was finding that cold, dark winter nights brought the highest demands from his consumers, while demand during the summer was almost nonexistent. Thus the additional generating capacity needed for peak load would lie dormant for most of the year. If Couch was going to develop his company in a cost-effective manner, he needed to find a way to equalize peak load over a twelve-month period.

Rice had first been brought to Arkansas by William Fuller of Carlisle, Arkansas, who had seen successful rice farms on a hunting trip to Louisiana in 1897. After several failures he went back to Louisiana to learn more about the new crop. He returned in 1903 to Carlisle to try again. Believing that lack of water had caused his earlier problem, he raised a thousand dollars from his neighbors and put in a 150-foot artesian well with a pump powered by steam. In the spring of 1904 he planted seventy acres. The yield was 5,225 bushels—almost 75 bushels per acre. This amazed his neighbor–investors. Rice was in Arkansas to stay.

Rice mushroomed as the choice of crops for farmers in the delta plain between the Arkansas and White Rivers. From the first spring in 1904 when a little over 5,000 bushels of crops were harvested, the crop continued to flourish, until by 1920 over 8.5 million bushels were harvested.

Rice was planted from the first of April until mid-May. After the first three weeks of growth, water was pumped over the crop to a depth of about six inches. Pumps, then, were critical to a successful Arkansas rice crop, but too often the oil/steam–powered pumps broke, causing delays in working the fields. Couch knew that the present pumps were unsatisfactory, but he also knew that convincing farmers to switch to more expensive, untried, electric pumps would be difficult.

To overcome any reluctance on the part of the rice farmers, Couch developed an aggressive marketing strategy. Arkansas

Light and Power began to promote electric pumps as a more reliable alternative to the present system. Couch's company made the pumps even more attractive by financing their purchase with loans that did not have to be repaid till the fall harvest. His plan worked. Rice farmers across Arkansas's delta plain began to switch to electric pumps. Buoyed by the success of this campaign, Couch began a similar program to electrify the ginning and compressing operations of cotton farmers.

As summertime demand grew, Couch was now in a position to increase the production capability of Arkansas Light and Power. A new plant in the same region of this cotton and rice activity would allow electric demand to grow at a steady pace. There were two plants already in operation that were likely prospects, one in Little Rock, the other in Pine Bluff. The controllers of the Little Rock plant did not want to sell, but Pine Bluff did. Couch quickly acquired the plant, which was now the most technically sophisticated plant in the AL&P system.

The large Pine Bluff Company immediately became the jewel of Couch's organization. He decided to move his headquarters from Arkadelphia to Pine Bluff. The *Pine Bluff Graphic* announced the news on the front page of its July 13, 1917, issue. It also stated that Couch would be also be leaving his new $10,000 home in Arkadelphia and bringing his family with the company. Couch, the paper said, would be bringing men "alert and keen; men who are great assets for the city." Jessie Couch said they were moving as much as a Methodist minister's family.

Even with this large acquisition, Couch continued to buy electric service franchises by the fistful. Stuttgart, Clarendon, Carlisle, England, Blytheville, and Rector were added, and others seemed to join AL&P's list almost daily.

As this astounding growth continued, Couch's administrative abilities were being promoted by newspapers across the state. By 1917, the United States was involved in the World War that had been wrecking Europe since 1914. A nationwide fuel shortage required each state to appoint a "fuel administrator" to assume czar-like powers over fuel distribution and pricing in their state. On November 1, 1917, President Woodrow Wilson, on the recommendation of Governor Charles H. Brough of Arkansas, appointed Couch Fuel Administrator for the State of Arkansas. This tribute to Couch's abilities was surprising, since he was a

Pine Bluff Power Plant

Pine Bluff at about the time Couch moved his offices there

fuel supplier himself by virtue of having the Russellville coal plant. Couch, however, immediately lived up to this trust by gathering coal suppliers from the state in his office and ordering a price reduction of coal from 50 to 25 cents per ton.

During the remainder of the war, even while his company was facing its most critical expansion period, Couch actively oversaw the distribution and supply of fuel across the state. On one visit to a coal yard, he was surprised to find a large stack of coal lying at a far corner of a mine field. He asked the owner why it wasn't being used.

"It's waste, not high enough quality."

"If I find a market for it, will you split a portion of the profits with the Fuel Administrator's office?"

"Sure, but there's no market."

Couch was back the next week with a buyer for the low-grade coal. By the end of the war $28,000 had been paid as commission to the Fuel Administrator's office. Couch tried to turn the money over to the federal government and was told there were no procedures for accepting money like this. He then turned the money over to the State of Arkansas. In turn, the state wanted Couch to accept $2,500 for his services as administrator. Couch refused to accept for himself, but gave the money to Pine Bluff for a memorial for the veterans of the World War.

Couch hoped the end of the war would also provide relief for his financially troubled company. Though wartime had created a sharp increase in demand for electric power, rates had been frozen as part of the war effort. Electric growth had required additional investment, but for every dollar of additional revenue from customers, five or six dollars had had to go into plant and equipment purchases. On December 31, 1919, the cash balance of Arkansas Light and Power stood at $1,171, compared to accounts payable of $374,715. Common stockholders were not realizing any dividends. Couch sold his home in Arkadelphia and put the money into the company; he refused to draw a salary; and he sold some of the northern property of the company. In desperation, he also applied for a general rate increase to the Arkansas Corporation Commission, newly formed and empowered to review such requests. They quickly recognized the need and the request was granted. Couch's home town of Magnolia objected to the increase, so Couch sold his franchise back to the town. When the citizens found they could not get power any more cheaply, they asked to be brought back into the AL&P system.

As the twenties began, Couch was beginning to see improvement in the company's financial picture. By December 31, 1922, the company was furnishing retail electric service to 35 towns in Arkansas and wholesale service to twelve others. It was also in charge of water service to nine towns and ice service to three. The company had a transmission network of 400 miles, and net income had increased to $254,228.

This decade was bringing changes to America. The influx of young men back from the war was affecting the culture of the country. Their experiences in Europe had broadened their outlook. Former soldiers were starting families, joining the work force, and becoming consumers, seemingly all at once. Wartime shortages had created a tremendous pent-up demand, and the recession that occurred right after the end of the First World War was over. Now the step of the country noticeably quickened. America could finally enjoy the changes the twentieth century had brought. One major innovation in American life was just coming into use across the country—the radio.

Harvey Couch was on a trip to Pittsburgh in 1920 when he heard his first radio program. He was immediately impressed by its capabilities. Here was his opportunity to tell his message of opportunity in Arkansas to more people than he could tell personally. On his return to Arkansas he immediately ordered a radio set for his family.

When the set arrived, it was a strange addition to the Couch home. Radios were owned only by a few scattered individuals who had the patience to dial slowly and carefully in search of the few broadcast stations in the major cities. In fact, Couch had his radio for several days before he could pick up anything on it. One Sunday afternoon, after his wife had left for the evening with the children, he sat down once again to begin his lonely vigil in front on the lighted dial on the radio. He twisted the dial knob till he found the location of the Pittsburgh station. He went outside and rotated the roof antenna, and then returned and began to move the dial as slowly as he could while listening intently to the roar of the static. Suddenly, "This is the Westinghouse Electric and Manufacturing Company at East Pittsburgh talking," came through his headset. Couch pulled the headset off and turned around to see who had entered the room. Just as quickly he realized what had happened: his radio had finally worked! He grabbed at the headset and listened. "This is KDKA signing off. Good night." The radio station was leaving the air for the evening, but its effect on Couch would not leave.

Over the next few months, while Couch was working on new construction projects for AL&P, his mind was still consumed with the possibilities of a radio station based in Arkansas. Westinghouse was using radio to promote its products; why couldn't Couch use it to promote Arkansas? Couch met William Jennings Bryan, who told him that if there had been "radio telephony" when he first ran for the presidency, the speeches he would have made would have carried him to the White House.

Couch wanted to build a station in Arkansas, but first he had to create a market for the new medium. He began to donate radio sets to hospitals and prisons. In November 1921, Couch broadcast a trial program to the Rotary Club at the Pines Hotel in Pine Bluff. He installed two 100-foot poles, 50 feet apart, outside his house. After the Rotary Club had gathered, Couch introduced the radio and told what it could do for Arkansas. Then he turned on the set as the Rotarians listened breathlessly. Misses Ernestine and Ailec Norris broadcast several vocal and piano selections from Couch's living room directly over the air to the Hotel Pines. The program was completed with the playing of Victrola records. At the end of the program, at a perfectly timed dramatic moment, Couch announced that he would build Arkansas's first radio station and operate it out of his offices. As the applause subsided, the club members pushed toward the radio to touch its dial and talk to Couch about which would be the best type to buy. The Pines immediately bought one and set it up in its lobby to entertain guests. Radio stations were going on the air across America; it seemed everyone wanted a radio.

J.L. Longino had studied radio in college, so he was given the responsibility of overseeing the construction of the radio station. He felt the call letters of the new station should "stand for something" so he dubbed the new station WOK for "Workers of Kilowatts." Ralph Pittman, the company's electrical superintendent began the hands-on construction of WOK.

On February 18, 1922, WOK was ready for broadcast. Couch

A.G. Whidden at microphone for Arkansas's first radio station, WOK

had been selling sets from the Pine Bluff Company's office. Ralph Pittman was given the honor of being the first on the air from the 500-watt station. On the first night Pittman made announcements called "Bulletins." Local listeners were urged to call the company telephone number to comment on reception. The station began with regular programs every Tuesday and Friday evening. Al Whidden, the new advertising manager of Arkansas Light and Power, assumed the microphone responsibility. The programs varied: Victrola records, live studio entertainment, and baseball scores made up most of the material. When Ralph Lee, inventor of the electric washing machine, visited Pine Bluff in March on a promotional tour, Couch put him on the radio. Lee proved to be a capable performer. He sang several songs and then talked about the advantages of the electric washing machine to the "economy, health, and work of the home."

Couch was using the station to sell, but his main product was Arkansas. He wrote an article for *Radio Topics* in which he said, "It is giving us an opportunity to advertise Arkansas in a way that it has never been advertised before." He was right. As Al Whidden was proclaiming over the airwaves the beauty of the state and the industry of its people, listeners wrote to the new station from as far north as the Canadian border, as far east as Long Island, and as far south as the Mexican border. They were hearing about Arkansas, most for the first time. Couch received a letter from the manager of a hotel in West Baden, Indiana, which said they "were entertaining hundreds of their guests" every Tuesday and Friday with programs from Arkansas. Shortly after the station opened, Couch wrote a letter to Elizabeth Keyser, a friend from Kansas City, in which he described his dream for the "wireless telephone" in Arkansas:

> One of the recent additions to our business is the wireless telephone. We are finding it very interesting, novel, and entertaining. We have a receiving set in our house where we hear concerts put on in Pittsburgh, New York, Detroit, Washington, and other places, with the clearness of a Victrola in your home. We have just installed a sending station of our own and are beginning to broadcast music, lectures, weather and market reports all over Arkansas and the adjoining teritory. We are now

receiving cards and letters from parties who have heard us far away as northern Wisconsin, Kansas, and Ohio. Last Friday evening, Miss Lenora Sparks, the Metropolitan Opera star, entertained the State Convention of the Musical Coterie at the Opera House here, and after the entertainment she came by and sent out three songs for us.

The wireless telephone is going to be a great benefit to mankind, especially in the rural districts where communication is difficult, besides the pleasure and profit the aged and infirm will derive from it. They can remain at home and listen in on good sermons, music, and entertainments in the larger cities. The closer we are able to bring the people of the world together and to a better understanding, the better place in which it will be to live. We are glad to do this for our own edification, and because of the fact it brings Pine Bluff before the entire Southwest; and since Pine Bluff had been good to me, we are glad to render this service.

For the next two years, until Couch sold the station to other interests, listeners heard the story of how Couch was helping build Arkansas and beginning to expand to other states.

With the post-war boom in full swing, Couch was now able to realize several long-standing dreams almost simultaneously. He was able to formalize plans for the hydroelectric development of the Ouachita River, purchase an additional power plant near Little Rock, and begin to acquire properties in Mississippi for his expanding electric system.

Since the days when he had explored the banks of the Ouachita with Flave Carpenter, Couch had been waiting for Arkansas's electric demand to climb high enough to warrant starting the first of three hydroelectric dams he wanted to build. As the decade began, it was obvious that Arkansas was ready for the first, smallest dam.

Over the previous years, Couch had had several engineering firms study the Ouachita and its potential as a source of hydroenergy. The concensus was that the river could support three dams designed so that the lake from one dam would come only to the foot of the next dam, rather than forming dam-to-dam lakes. With his blueprints and plans in hand, Couch headed for Washington to gain approval for what was to be one of the nation's most ambitious dam projects.

On his arrival in Washington, Couch found himself lost in the government bureaucracy. Unlike business, government was an organization in which no one seemed capable of making a decision alone. Couch moved from committee to committee, learning the ropes. As he began to sort through the tangle of offices and procedures, he discovered that, indeed, one man could make the decision as to his dam project. Secretary of War John Weeks was in charge of the commission that could approve Couch's proposal, but he was leaving for an extended trip to Alaska.

Couch was desperate. He knew his New York financing was precarious at best. A delay in beginning his dam project might make his New York investors pull out of the deal and prevent his hydro-dreams from being realized for years to come. Couch returned to his Washington hotel to consider his alternatives. As he entered the lobby he ran into Colonel H.L. Remmel. Couch then told him his story and asked for suggestions for a course of action. Remmel was a staunch Arkansas Republican who knew Weeks personally. Remmel asked Couch to come with him, and they turned around and headed for Secretary Weeks's office.

Weeks's office was filled with people trying to see the secretary before he left on his trip. Weeks was seeing no one else. Remmel insisted that his card be presented to the secretary, and the two men took a seat. The card had immediate effect. Remmel and Couch were politely ushered into the office of the Secretary of War.

The three men sat down and made small talk for only a moment. Then Couch, who had seen many exercises in financial power, saw an impressive display of political power.

"Harvey Couch is a friend of mine and a Democrat," Remmel said, "but good enough to be a Republican. He wants to build a dam in Arkansas and wants you to hold a meeting of the Commission Monday so a license can be granted."

"Mr. Couch,"—Weeks turned toward Couch—"are your papers filled out and ready?"

"Yes, sir. Everything is in good shape and ready for examination."

"All right." Weeks turned back toward Remmel. "Colonel, you have never failed me, and I won't fail you. This meeting will

Surveying party for Remmel Dam

Remmel Dam under construction

No.3 #
PHOTO BY
TOO CUTE STUDIO
HOT SPRINGS ARK.

be held Monday morning and the license will be granted."

Couch couldn't believe his ears. He had been prepared for days of extensive interviews. He numbly shook Secretary Weeks's hand and walked out of the office with Colonel Remmel.

After Couch and Remmel were back at the hotel, Couch searched for some way to show his appreciation. Only one thing seemed appropriate.

"Colonel, you have done me a great favor, and to express my appreciation that dam will be called 'Remmel Dam.'"

The first campsite at Remmel Dam was set up nine miles from Malvern in May 1923, with actual construction beginning in August 1923. John Nickerson, a New York investor, had formed the association which funded the $2.5 million for the building of the dam. He made frequent trips to Arkansas to inspect its progress. He was impressed with the economy with which Couch was insuring that nothing was wasted during construction. The wood for the frame was taken from trees in the soon-to-be lake bed, sand and gravel for cement was taken from the stream bed, and scraps from the workers' lunches were used to feed hogs that were then butchered for the men.

Couch frequently brought newpaper reporters to the site to show them the progress. All of Arkansas would benefit from Remmel Dam, Couch told them, with 300 miles of transmission lines being added to the AL&P system to carry Remmel power throughout the state.

By December 1924 the 9,000-kilowatt dam was completed. Couch brought hundreds of guests and reporters by train to inspect the new dam. It was 900 feet long and 65 feet high and was the most modern electric production facility in the state. It had formed a lake of about 2,000 acres which Couch had named after his only daughter, Catherine. She had been born in 1918 and a fourth son, William, in 1919.

Several months later, Pat Neff, Couch's former teacher and until recently the governor of Texas, had the opportunity to visit Remmel Dam with Harvey Couch. As the two men walked across the walkway on top of the dam, they fell into a pleasant argument.

"Neff," Harvey said, "had it had not been for you, this dam would never have been built."

"Oh, yes it would, Harvey. You would have built it!"

Harvey Couch in the early 1920s

"No, you really built this dam. If it had not been for you I would probably even now be working at the gin in Calhoun."

Neff shook his head, and the two men fell silent. As they looked across Lake Catherine, Harvey Couch was standing on top of the world—standing on Remmel Dam.

At the same time Remmel Dam was being realized, Couch was beginning his expansion plans in Mississippi. That state was much like Arkansas, poor and rural. But Mississippi did not have one thing that Arkansas did—Harvey Couch. Each community was still relying on its own power station, and the dependability of each system varied wildly. If Mississippi was to expand its production capability it would need to develop an interconnected system much like the one Couch was developing in Arkansas.

In 1922, Couch visited the lawyer Garner Green, Sr., of Jackson, Mississippi. He wanted Green to become the legal representative for his company in that state. Couch told him he intended to develop an interconnected system in Mississippi. Couch continued, "Our company doesn't have any money right now, and won't for some time, but we'll treat you right." Green accepted this offhand proposal, hired on with Couch, and began to look for acquisitions in the state. Properties were soon located in Jackson, Vicksburg, Columbus, and Greenville. With money from Couch's old "New York connection" these properties were purchased and incorporated April 12, 1923, as Mississippi Power and Light.

Couch sent his younger brother, Pete, to supervise operations at the new company. There was much work to do: existing facilities needed to be improved and a major power source sufficient to attract new industry to Mississippi had to be developed. That power source, it would turn out, would emerge not in Mississippi or Arkansas, but in the third state in which Couch wanted to expand.

The discovery of what was called "the north Louisiana field" of natural gas—considered to be the world's largest—changed Couch's plans. Originally, he had intended to build a major new coal-fired plant in Russellville to provide service to his expanding system. But the Louisiana discovery made him think about a different fuel source. At first Couch considered having the low-cost natural gas transported to Camden where he had enough property to build a plant, but the cost was prohibitive. He finally decided to build the plant in Sterlington, Louisiana, in the heart of the north Louisiana field.

Couch quickly formed the Louisiana Power Company and approached John Nickerson of New York once again for funding. The estimated cost of the 30,000-kilowatt plant plus transmission lines was about $5 million. Nickerson and his consortium agreed to sell $2.25 million in bonds if Couch would provide an equal amount as equity capital. Couch had stretched his finances to the limit by expanding as quickly as he had in Arkansas and Mississippi, and did not have anthing close to that in money or unencumbered property. No other funding source would provide Couch with additional money. Harvey Couch was beat...except that he refused to be beat.

Couch boarded a train for Pittsburgh with AL&P's lawyer Hamilton Moses. They had scheduled an appointment with James Guy Tripp, chairman of the board of Westinghouse Electric and Manufacturing Company. They spent the day with Tripp, examining maps and engineer reports on the proposed Sterlington plant. Tripp seemed excited by the possibilities for the plant. After lunch Couch made his proposal.

"Mr. Tripp, we want to buy all of our generating equipment from you. We want to build the most modern, cheapest-producing station in the South at Sterlington. It's going to be a beauty! It will add to your reputation. We want a great big plaque with a big letter 'W' on it to be displayed so that everybody in the trains and everybody that passes Sterlington can see that plaque and think of Westinghouse. Then, if you will let us, we want a big fine picture of James Guy Tripp in the building." Couch took a breath. "We want you to sell us all this equipment on credit, and then waive your lien so we can mortgage the property and sell bonds for the funds to finish the work. In other words, we want you to furnish the equity money."

Tripp did not blink.

"Mr. Couch, you are making a strange request. I doubt if we have ever done anything like that; in fact, I doubt if we have ever before had such a request. Yet, we appreciate the business your company has been giving us. I believe in your plans and in the future of your company and that territory."

Tripp paused and rubbed his hand on his chin. He looked

out the window, was quiet for a long moment, and then turned back toward Couch.

"I know you're having a hard time getting this equity money. I'll ask our board to give you a line of credit for a million dollars with which you can purchase our equipment, and we'll waive our lien and take your open notes in payment. We'll give you three years to pay us. In the meantime, go ahead and issue your bonds for your senior finances."

The next day, Couch and Moses went to see Colonel Davis, who ran the Aluminum Company of America. They wanted about a million dollars' worth of aluminum conductors under the same arrangements they had gotten at Westinghouse. After several hours of going over their plans with Davis, they made their proposal.

Davis, unlike Tripp, blinked.

"Why, Mr. Couch, I never heard of anything like that," he sputtered. "I doubt if any such thing has ever been done!"

"Just a minute," Couch interrupted. "We've just made such an arrangement with Mr. Tripp of Westinghouse. He is going to sell us all of our equipment for our plant on the same basis, and on the terms of three years."

Davis sat back in his chair. He smiled and shook his head.

"We believe in you as much as Tripp does. We'll give you whatever you need."

Sterlington was put into operation in November 1925. In design and intent it could fairly be called Couch's first power plant of the twentieth century. It had the largest capacity of any power plant south of St. Louis. His previous plants were improvements in the electric plant designs of the late nineteenth century. Sterlington was designed as the major electricity producer of an interconnected, interstate system. Its capacity was divided by its three owners, Arkansas Light and Power, Mississippi Power and Light, and Louisiana Power Company. All of Couch's previous plants had been built near towns or cities; Sterlington, however, was built near the fuel source, away from towns, and hard to reach over country dirt roads. The community of Sterlington was more of a crossroads and could not handle the influx of plant personnel. In order to provide for the workers of Sterlington, Couch decided to build a company town.

The village Couch constructed for the 48 worker families

was grander than anything within miles. It had a sewage system, concrete sidewalks, graveled streets, and electric, water, and gas service. Couch also built a school and church. A nurse was brought in to provide for the medical needs of the workers and their families, with a doctor scheduled for regular visits.

The single men—fifteen to twenty in number—were housed in a boardinghouse known as "the Club," which was run by a couple who provided meals to the boarders. They also tended the Club's dairy herd, vegetable garden, and chickens.

All the workers wore clean white uniforms and worked ten-hour days. Any problems in the community were brought to the station superintendent, who acted as mayor and sheriff for the village.

At the dedication of the Sterlington plant, Governor Harvey Parnell of Arkansas said, "Harvey Couch has done more to develop these three states—Louisiana, Arkansas, and Mississippi—than any other man." Harvey Couch controlled an electric empire that covered three states. He had put together deals totaling millions of dollars. It would be difficult, if not impossible, for anyone in the audience at that dedication to realize that Harvey Couch was still personally approving any purchase over $10, and that any miscalculation in finances or projected electrical growth could plunge his system into the darkness of bankruptcy almost overnight.

Couch at dedication of the Sterlington plant

Chapter Five

DURING THE ENTIRE history of Arkansas Light and Power, Couch
was continually trying to locate additional capital to help build
his system. Except for Banker's Trust, run by his friend Charlie
McCain, the big Little Rock banks were not supportive of Couch's
grand industrialization projects. The *Pine Bluff Graphic* had
reported on December 28, 1920:

> It is the ambition of the head of the company to
> provide for Arkansas...huge central stations and send
> power over a network of high voltage lines to all cities and
> communities in the section...[M]any millions would be
> needed for the development.

To make this pledge come true, Couch was spending more and
more time in New York trying to locate investors.

In Arkansas, Couch used the financial boosterism of
ex–railroad man, now AL&P executive, Louis Garrett. Garrett
was as extroverted as Couch, and as determined to see AL&P
grow as a major utility. When Couch's expansion drained AL&P's
resources, Garrett would grab a handful of stocks and head out
on a stock-selling spree. He would find some of his old railroad
friends who could always be counted on to purchase some stock.

Garrett also managed the sometimes meager company
funds in the same aggressive manner. If money was tight at Pine

Bluff, Garrett would write a draft on a distant local office for an amount he thought was reasonable for that office to have on hand. He would cash a draft on that local manager at a local bank. When the draft arrived at that local office, the office manager would pay it. If he could not, the draft was returned to the home office, where Garrett would have sold enough stocks to pay for the draft.

The feast-and-famine cycle continued through AL&P's early years. As soon as Couch acquired a new system he would be faced with the expensive proposition of replacing that community's outdated equipment. Once when Couch did not have enough funds to connect his system with Altheimer, the residents of the town went out and bought enough stock in AL&P to pay for the construction of an extension of lines to their community.

Couch, meanwhile, was making more and more frequent trips to New York City in search of financing. He was driven to expand the electric production capability in the three states his company served. New industries, and the jobs that came with them, could be attracted to the South only by readily available electric energy, he believed. His time, however, was becoming completely dominated by these New York excursions. Returning to Arkansas by train, he hit upon the idea of bringing New York investors to Arkansas. This would save him some time, and, he hoped, would make selling Arkansas easier.

Couch brought his first trainload of New York investors to Arkansas in June 1921. Although Couch was well known to these men, Arkansas was not. Couch personally guided the businessmen to the spots he felt best represented the potential of Arkansas. Couch was pleased when one of the bankers returned to New York and wrote a short article on the trip for the *New York Tribune*. He stated, "I found Arkansas a much different state than I supposed it to be—a state of wonderful and varied resources and in the cities visited a pushing, energetic and hopeful lot of businessmen." Harvey Couch couldn't have said it better himself.

Arkansas Light and Power employees were working 55 to 60 hours a week in order to keep up with the rapid expansion. Couch was driving himself no less hard; he had not taken a vacation since forming the company in 1913. What he was doing, creating an interstate utility with relatively little start-up capital,

MERCHANDISE STATEMENT

ARKANSAS LIGHT & POWER COMPANY

Dunkley Ark., *8/15* 192*4*

SOLD TO *Dr E D McKnight*   Bill No. *24*

Your Order No.

·ADDRESS   Job Ticket No.

75'	#14 R C wire	@ .0?		1 50
30'	Fixture Cord	@ .03		90
2'	Drop Cord	@ .05		10
12	Knobs	@ .03		36
20'	Loom	@ .05		1 00
5	Key Sockets	@ .50		2 50
7	Drop Chain	@ .15		1 05
4	Cut outs	@ 70		80
1	Consolidated Rosette	@ 35		35
1	Bryant Push Switch			50
			TOTAL	9 06

PLEASE BRING THIS BILL WITH YOU

MERCHANDISE STATEMENT

ARKANSAS LIGHT & POWER COMPANY

Dunkley Ark., *8/15* 192*4*

SOLD TO *E D McKnight*   Bill No. *28*

Your Order No.

ADDRESS   Job Ticket No.

1	Pump Switch Cover			10
1	Switch Box = Base supplies			35
8	Fixture Loops	@ .03		24
	8½ hrs labor		8	50
			TOTAL	9 19

PLEASE BRING THIS BILL WITH YOU

Two invoices for completely wiring a new home—a duty of Arkansas Light and Power linemen in 1924—at a cost of about $9.00 for parts and $8.50 for 8 1/2 hours of labor was unique in America. Most of the large investors were saying it was only a matter of time before Couch and AL&P overextended themselves and were forced to quit business. One New York utility tycoon in particular, Sydney Z. Mitchell of the giant Electric Bond and Share Company, was waiting for Harvey Couch (as he told his associates) "to hang himself."

Sydney Zollicoffer Mitchell had been born in Alabama in 1862. He had studied the principles of electricity at the United States Naval Academy. While in the service of the U.S. Navy, he had begun the electrical wiring of warships in the fleet. Upon leaving the service he went to work for Edison General Electric Company, which primarily manufactured electrical equipment. His duties for them were to acquire and run small electric companies that ran into financial trouble. As the industry began to expand, Edison General Electric merged with another company and became General Electric. After seeing Mitchell's success in acquiring and managing small electric companies, General Electric decided in 1905 to form a new subsidiary for the purpose of acquiring companies on a nationwide scale with Mitchell as its head.

The Electric Bond and Share Company then began doing what Couch would later do in Arkansas—acquiring scattered utility companies and interconnecting them for greater efficiency. With the financial troubles that new electric companies were undergoing across the country, Mitchell had no trouble finding properties to acquire. Soon Electric Bond and Share had become the major electric holding company in the nation, with properties from San Diego to the Bronx. Mitchell did not have the financial worries that Couch had in beginning his system, since he had the backing of the nation's largest manufacturer of electrical equipment. Savings from the interconnection of power were immediate, allowing Mitchell's operations to grow at a tremendous rate. By 1925, the Electric Bond and Share Company had acquired more than 100 companies and had a total invested capital of about $650 million.

During the early part of the 1920s Couch and Mitchell were beginning to have skirmishes, for Mitchell was expanding his holdings into the Middle South. When the Little Rock property was put up for sale in 1923, Mitchell's greater financial resources allowed him to acquire the system before Couch could arrange for financing.

With his acquisition of the Little Rock business, Mitchell wanted to build an interconnected system in the remaining Arkansas communities not part of Couch's AL&P. In February 1926, he and Couch again went head to head in the unlikely battleground of Wynne, Arkansas. Wynne became not just another city whose electric franchise was up for purchase, but a test of strength for the two rival organizations. Both companies sent representatives to speak before the Wynne City Council.

The spokesmen for Electric Bond and Share went first. Theirs was a well-organized, impressive display of charts, statistics, and the company's track record. These men from New York had made similar proposals before city councils throughout America. Their presentation was almost overwhelming in displaying what this multimillion dollar organization could do for the tiny town of Wynne, Arkansas. In conclusion they produced checks from AL&P that had been returned for insufficient funds. The message for the city council was clear. The men sat down. They had created the desired effect; the room was quiet. It was obvious that they knew what they were doing.

Harvey Couch had sent Hamilton Moses as the representative from Arkansas Light and Power. All eyes were on him as he began. First he admitted that AL&P had some checks returned recently, but the bills corresponding to them had all been paid. The problem occurred because Harvey Couch was keeping rates as low as possible for Arkansans, and this sometimes made money tight for the company.

He then had a series of questions for the council. He knew they all had heard of Harvey Couch, but had any one of them ever heard of S. Z. Mitchell? Had Mr. Mitchell ever done anything for Arkansas? If they had a problem with their utility they could drive to Pine Bluff and talk to Harvey Couch about it personally; did they think they would be able to drive to New York City and talk to Mr. Mitchell? Would they even be able to find Mr. Mitchell? Harvey Couch had been serving without a salary to "help build Arkansas." He had sold his home and put the money into the company. He had dedicated his life to Arkansas. Which man would be more concerned with the welfare of a small town in Arkansas?

As he finished, Moses returned to his seat and gave a brief

smile to the Electric Bond and Share representatives. When the council voted it was unaminous: Wynne, Arkansas, would become part of the Arkansas Light and Power system. Hamilton Moses knew what he was doing also.

It was obvious to Couch that he could not afford to continue to fight a company with unlimited resources. He might be able to win each seperate battle, but the cost of bidding against Mitchell in each town would lose him the war. Another factor was playing on Couch's mind. He was 48 years old. His black hair was now mixed evenly with grey. His priorities in life had not changed dramatically, but they had subtly evolved. His purpose in life was to build; if he could be a better builder by tying in with Electric Bond and Share, then his course of action was clear to him. Mitchell typically allowed the management of companies that he acquired to remain in place. With Mitchell's money at his disposal, he could do even more to "help build Arkansas." A meeting was arranged between Couch and Mitchell in New York City.

The *Pine Bluff Graphic* announced the deal on October 3, 1926. The front page story was headlined, "Combination Headed by Couch and Longino Formed to Give Arkansas Huge Linked Electrical Resources." It continued:

> Merger of the Arkansas Light and Power Company, the Arkansas Central Power Company, the Pine Bluff company and a group of other public service properties in Arkansas into the Arkansas Power and Light Company, headed by H.C. Couch, was made known today with the filing of articles of incorporation of the new company in the office of the secretary of state.
>
> With a capital of 1,300,000 shares of no par value common stock and 250,000 shares of no par value preferred stock, the Arkansas Power and Light Company is the largest company ever incorporated in Arkansas. The incorporation fee alone is $32,500, which goes into the general revenue fund of the state. The company could have been incorporated in Delaware, it was pointed out, for a fee of about $4,000, but the incorporators, loyal to Arkansas, preferred to pay the difference to make it an Arkansas company in every sense.

The merger would allow instant interconnection for much

Little Rock offices of AP&L, showing Harvey Couch's second-floor office at the 4th and Louisiana corner of the building

of the state. It would also be important for Couch's Mississippi Power and Light and Louisiana Power Company, which was incoporated as Louisiana Power and Light under the new holding company called the Electric Power and Light Company. Mitchell controlled the New Orleans electric system, and that was brought into the holding company. With the addition of needed capital rapid expansion could begin in all three states. In fact, Couch was already beginning to badger Mitchell about needed funds for development of electric power in his territory. He reported Mitchell's response to the *Pine Bluff Graphic*:

> Couch, that family of properties you have back home in the south are increasing like guinea pigs, and they are hungry rascals. You are going to "get me in bad" with some of our connections by letting you have all the money we have here, but I love the south and have great faith in its future. How much do you need this time?

A lot, as it turned out. Over the next five years Couch and Arkansas Power and Light would add 52 systems serving 115 communities to their system; by 1931 they were supplying 228 communities with electric power. Mitchell grew to trust Couch's judgement implicitly. Although he had assigned a special "sponsor" to give the Electric Bond and Share Company the final word on company decisions, the sponsor never exercised his authority. At board meetings of Arkansas Power and Light in New York City Couch acted as chairman. On June 25, 1929, Mitchell spoke at a testimonial dinner in honor of Couch. Mitchell, who was notorious for never leaving his New York office, had traveled all the way to Arkansas to pay tribute to his new friend. He said:

> He dreams dreams that always come true. I regard him as the most practical constructive genius that the South and West have ever produced. He is practical because his plans are sound, and he always knows how to get money to put them through. He is so human that nobody can know him without loving him. I am proud to be associated with him.

Mitchell joined a chorus of Arkansas voices in praise of Couch. Newspapers were referring to him as Arkansas's "First Citizen."

Arkansas Power and Light was bringing dependable electric energy to small towns across Arkansas, some for the first time. But even more important to the audience at the tribute in Pine Bluff, Harvey Couch had just led the state through the worst disaster in the history of Arkansas.

Heavy winter rain began falling in Arkansas in December 1926. There was nothing unusual about this; rain is a part of every Arkansas winter. What was unusual was the amounts and duration. From December 1926 to April 1927 heavy rain continued up and down the Mississippi Valley.

During the first week of April, nine inches of rain fell across Arkansas, eight to nine inches fell into the Arkansas River in Oklahoma, and more than six inches fell into the Mississippi River in Kansas. By the second week of April it was certain that a flood was going to occur, but where and how severe it would be was uncertain.

On Friday, April 15, 1927, the worst predictions were not realized; rather, what happened was beyond anyone's expectations. The Mississippi jumped its banks with almost incredible force and fury. In a short time about 26,000 square miles in seven states were covered by the muddy river, with over 5,289,576 acres of farmland destroyed. Total damages of the flood were later estimated by the American Red Cross as $236,334,414. The Red Cross also reported the loss of 246 lives.

Bruce Catton, the historian, surveyed the damage:

> Southern financiers estimate it will take five years for the South to recover from this blow; that the flood is the greatest in history; that the reconstruction problem the valley will face when the flood subsides will be as serious as anything the South has faced since the reconstruction days after the Civil War.

The state of Arkansas was hit worst by the disaster.

Herbert Hoover, Secretary of Commerce under President Calvin Coolidge, was placed in charge of relief efforts. He visited Arkansas in late April to gauge the situation. He told Governor John E. Martineau to appoint a Flood Relief Director for the state, saying:

> I suggest three things to bring about relief: first, organiza-
> tion; second, organization; third, organization. The orga-
> nization in each state should attack the problem
> thoroughly and diligently, first determining the amount
> of relief needed, and then supplying the need.

There was only one man in the state capable of creating such order out of chaos. On April 31, 1927, Martineau appointed Harvey Couch as director of flood relief for the State of Arkansas. Couch would also supervise the rescue activities of the Arkansas Red Cross.

Couch now had two disaster-related chores—relieving the flood woes of the people of Arkansas and providing power to the three states in his system all hit hard by the flood.

To a large extent, providing power to flood areas was made possible by interconnection. Couch's dream and purpose of providing Arkansas with an interconnected system was proving itself in a most dramatic way. Before his system, power to individual towns was provided by plants inside the towns themselves. Those towns in the flood area would have been without electricity for weeks, had the interconnected system not been in use. The Little Rock plant, for example, was completely flooded when a sewer pipe running underneath it burst, covering the plant in several feet of water. Its equipment was damaged and could not provide service to a town now dependent on electric energy, but because of the interconnection of the Arkansas Power and Light system Little Rock was kept "on line" for the duration of high waters.

Interconnection provided only part of the answer in restoring electric power after the flood. In areas under water, linemen used rowboats to reach inaccessible spots where they needed to raise transformers or repair broken wires. AP&L employees were risking their lives in the swirling, muddy waters. Frequently their boats would overturn, but they would climb back in, completely soaked, in temperatures cold for April, and continue on to correct a transmission problem. In areas where the poles were down they used iron pipes to mount the wires on until the water subsided.

Workers at Remmel Dam had their hands full also. The

Substation at Clarendon during the 1927 flood

Scott, Mississippi, May 10, 1927

Ouachita River was experiencing the greatest flow in its history. The plant, which had a 9,000-kilowatt capacity, was reduced to about 7,500 by the high waters. The crest of Remmel Dam is 290 feet high, the top of the gates are at 307 feet, and the walkway is at 315 feet. During the flood the river was 17 feet above the crest of the dam. Plant employees worked around the clock placing sandbags at each end of the dam to prevent water from washing away the land on either side. The crew also placed sandbags at the walkway to the dam to prevent water from rushing in the door and flooding the plant.

During one of the bad storms during the flood, the line from Remmel Dam to Little Rock went down. Workers from Remmel rode horseback through the high waters, working their way toward the site of the damage. Until they were able to finish their repair work, power from another part of the system was diverted to Little Rock—a maneuver that would not have been possible without an interconnected system.

The rice-growing areas along the White River were also hit hard. Rice fields became boat-covered lakes as people fled the rising waters. Clarendon was taken out of service deliberately, since the high waters came close to the wires strung on poles. Evacuees who might come into contact with the charged line were at risk. AP&L sent men by boat to cut the line and then reconnect the Clarendon system to power available from the old city generator. This power was then fed to the more important buildings in the town for the benefit of those who stayed in Clarendon.

Mississippi was also grateful for the benefits of interconnection. Greenville, Mississippi, was evacuated during the flood, but the new line from Greenville to the Sterlington plant stood, and continuous electric service was provided to the emptying town.

The efficiency of Couch's power companies impressed Herbert Hoover. He said:

> Had it not been for the transmission lines interconnecting the towns and cities of Arkansas and Mississippi, conditions would have been much worse, for no matter where people were forced to go by the floods, there they would find electric service and all of the comforts it implies.

During the flood, telephone service was erratic at best. To make a call from Pine Bluff to Brinkley, a distance of 90 miles, the caller had to be routed through St. Louis. Any break in AP&L's transmission lines might therefore go unreported for hours. To avoid the possibility of any break going undiscovered, seaplanes were commandeered from as far south as Florida to patrol the lines and also look for anyone stranded in the flood. There were hundreds of people who had been stranded on bridges, levees, and high ground across Arkansas; their safety was the responsibility of Harvey Couch.

The task undertaken by the Red Cross was simply herculean. The *Pine Bluff Graphic* reported that there were 100,000 people homeless in southeast Arkansas. Pine Bluff was completely covered in water. J.L. Longino was rehabilitation chairman of the Red Cross. His job was made more difficult working out of a flooded city, and also by the fact that many of the farm families resisted moving out until it was too late to effectively move them.

During the worst of the flood hundreds of people were stranded on the Free Bridge seven miles north of Pine Bluff. Tents were erected on the bridge to provide shelter for the homeless. But as the waters continued to advance, these refugees became marooned. Lula Toler, a rescue worker, reported:

> Women, with their babies in arms, men and women, bent with years, waited on the bridge casting wistful eyes to the land of safety, hungry, wet and tired through the long hours of the stormy night, listening to the dashing of the angry waves, watching the drowning of the cattle and the floating of their belongings.

To save them, a flotilla of hundreds of requisitioned fishing boats, old riverboats, and anything else that would float was gathered at the water in front of the Jefferson County Courthouse. Braving the rain and cold temperatures, relief workers rescued over 300 people from the bridge and took them to Red Cross relief centers set up by Longino.

This was the major instance of people's being marooned by the flood, but there were many other smaller versions played out across the southern part of the state. Airman Griff McSwine was flying a seaplane that Couch had requisitioned when he saw on a levee "fifty people waving at me [to]...hear their cries for help. It

Harvey Couch and Herbert Hoover meeting to confer about flood relief, 1927

was pitiful."

Couch and the Red Cross were scurrying to find homes for the ever-increasing homeless. An emergency camp near Forrest City held over 15,000 people homeless from the flood. Couch set up rescue centers in Crossett, Clarendon, Cotton Plant, and dozens of other towns in the southern part of the state. As Couch surveyed the camps it became obvious to him that reestablishing 100,000 people at their farms and homes would be a tremendous challenge. Their crops had been destroyed, their farm animals drowned, and their seed and supplies washed away. Herbert Hoover indicated that he did not think the economic relief of these people was the responsibility of the government, so the task fell to Couch to devise some type of rehabilitation system for these people. The system he devised was unique.

Couch formed a $1 million reconstruction corporation fund for the flood area. It would be funded by organizations that did business in that part of the country. He sent out 21 telegrams and received over $200,000 in reply. In addition, Arkansas Power and Light subscribed for $10,000, which was matched by Mississippi Power and Light, Louisiana Power and Light, and Electric Bond and Share. Soon after, people from around the country had subscribed to create a fund of $2.5 million. The corporation provided loans to thousands of farmers and others who had been washed out by the flood. The money made it possible for farmers in the three-state area to resume their lives. Couch planned to keep the remainder of the money in the corporation as a revolving fund for future disasters. But his plans were changed in the most unexpected way. The victims who had received the money, once they were reestablished, quickly turned around and repaid their loans. With the total amount then back in his hands, Couch repaid every subscriber to the relief corporation in full, and then dissolved the organization.

The flood had another effect on Arkansas. It brought the region to the attention of the nation. The *New York Herald* carried an article expressing surprise that Arkansas had such a well-developed electric system. The *Arkansas Gazette* carried a response on May 22, 1927:

> ...How it must have startled the staid New Yorker to learn that in such a backwoods state as Arkansas, they are using

electricity in their farming operations.

But that's all right. If the New Yorkers can be made to believe there is anything west of Manhattan but a wilderness their knowledge of geography will be greatly improved.

Although the press accounts of how Arkansas responded to the flood were positive, Couch was still fighting the ignorance of New York bankers and investors in trying to attract new industry to Arkansas. He was presented with another opportunity to influence the decision-makers when he heard that International Paper might build a mill in Camden. He approached the company's vice-president and urged him to consider Arkansas. The vice-president agreed, and when he came to Arkansas Couch put his own car and driver at the visitor's disposal. The vice-president agreed to put his next mill in Camden.

Couch was elated. But then R.J. Cullen, the manager of the mill at Bastrop, Louisiana, protested the decision, saying that it would be more economical to enlarge the Bastrop location. Couch now had a new selling job. He brought Cullen to Arkansas to show him the proposed location. Couch later recounted how he and several Arkansas friends made the deal.

> Mr. Cullen and I went out into the field [where the mill is now located] and walked back and forth. Suddenly he stopped and said, "I'll tell you what I will do. This is a good location and if you will build a gas line in here, sell us gas at certain prices and sell us power on the Bastrop basis, or near it, and will give us 160 acres of land here for the mill, we will build it right here."
>
> "Wait right here," I said to Cullen. Back I went to see Mr. Gaughan, who was sitting in the in the car with J.H. Meek. He thought the land, about 300 acres, could be purchased for $20,000. "All right," I said, "I'll underwrite one-fourth of it."
>
> He agreed to underwrite one-fourth and so did Jim Meek. We decided to take our chances on raising the rest downtown. The deal was closed, and the mill was built.

For a big business to care paternally for the welfare of the citizens in its service area was unheard of in Arkansas, and rare for the United States as a whole in 1927. On May 15 of that year

Forbes, the national business magazine, highlighted this unusual concern of Couch's for the people of Arkansas in an article entitled "Arkansas and the New Viewpoint."

...[P]reachers in their pulpits have been proclaiming the gospel of self-forgetful service. But it remains for such organizations as the Arkansas Power and Light Company to introduce the mechanism by which all the people in this new civilization may most efficiently serve all the people—a situation in which even self-interest demands that no one shall concentrate upon serving himself...

There has been no lack of neighborly feeling in the less developed sections of America. The criticism of them, if any, has usually been of a certain narrowness of outlook, a lack of interest in what is happening to human life beyond their territorial boundaries. Industrial development has tended to change this...Now, the coming of interconnected power plants and transmission systems seems to be completing the change...

Arkansas Power and Light, although not a giant corporation in the electric field, is one whose development will be watched most closely by all who are interested in the great change which is coming over the southland...

To the people of Arkansas, however, this means much more than that a prosperous industry has arisen in the state. It means that the whole state is entering a new era. Everybody is interested in the success of such an enterprise, for it can succeed only through endowing the people in the cities, towns and farms with power, and as the people are endowed with power, human life takes on new meaning.

An Arkansas store window promoting new electric appliances

Chapter Six

After the flood waters subsided into the Mississippi, Couch believed that Arkansas Power and Light would now be able to enjoy the prosperity that was sweeping the nation. Americans were enjoying an expansion without precedence in American history. Every economic statistic available encouraged Couch to think that the future of the electric industry was bright indeed.

The population of the United States had increased 62 percent from 1899 to 1929, and the number of wage earners had increased by 88 percent during this same period. In 1919, 32 percent of factory machinery was powered by electricity; by 1929 the figure was 49 percent. In fact, by 1929 the United States was producing more electric power than the rest of the world combined.

It was not industry or population growth alone which accounted for this tremendous growth. For the first time Americans were becoming consumers of products that were mass-produced and mass-marketed. The new Hollywood movies and more sophisticated consumer advertising were promoting a lifestyle that would have seemed unattainable only a few years before. Another novelty, credit purchasing, was making a variety of products from electric stoves to electric vacuum cleaners affordable to the middle-class purchaser. In 1922, there was virtually no money spent to advertise electric refrigerators, but by 1927 the yearly advertising budget had swelled to $1.5 million. The average electric consumption of the American home was 410 kilowatt-hours at the beginning of 1920; by the end of the decade it had grown to 774 kilowatt-hours.

Looking at these statistics, Couch realized that if his companies were to keep pace with America's growth, he would have to increase the production capability of his system. He decided to build another dam.

When Couch first formed his electric company, Flave Carpenter had led Couch and Longino on horseback as they looked for possible dam sites on the Ouachita. Carpenter believed in water power and convinced Couch that the Ouachita could support not just one but several water projects, which not only would supply the Couch system with power but would establish some fine recreational lakes as well. So Couch looked to future development based on Arkansas's most abundant resource—water. In 1926, engineers were looking at proposed or actual projects on the North Fork of the White River, the lower White, Arkansas, Buffalo, Little Red, and Little Missouri Rivers, and dozens of other streams which they estimated could create one million horsepower for the state.

Holding permits from Washington, Couch decided that the time was now right to construct the second of several dams he envisioned on the river. As was typical with Couch, he decided to name the dam and lake after people he felt were most instrumental in making them a reality. The new dam would be called Carpenter Dam after Flave Carpenter, with its associated lake named Lake Hamilton after his attorney Hamilton Moses.

Carpenter Dam would be ten miles upstream from Remmel Dam. Lake Hamilton would be 24 miles long, cover about 9,000 acres, and create 75,000 horsepower. This was sufficient to power 100 towns with populations of 10,000. Larger than Remmel, the new dam would be 115 feet high and 1,165 feet long at the apex. It was estimated that a crew of close to 1,000 men would be needed to complete the different phases of its construction.

A four-mile railroad spur was established at the beginning of 1929 to connect the dam to the Missouri Pacific line. Heavy excavation for permanent structures was begun in April of the same year. Like the materials for Remmel Dam, the gravel for the concrete was taken from the river bank and the wood for framework was taken from the lake bed area. Concrete was loaded a

*Harvey Couch (at center with hat in hand) and Flave Carpenter
(to Couch's right) during construction of Carpenter Dam*

Harvey Couch (right) and Pete Couch (left) in front of a
Louisiana and Arkansas Railroad car

yard at a time and poured into the forms. A total of 150,000 yards of concrete would be needed. The construction site was powered by transmission lines connected to Remmel Dam.

During the planning and construction of Carpenter Dam, Harvey Couch was riding a wave of popularity without precedent in Arkansas. Almost every day the newspapers carried stories on the local boy who had become a millionaire industrialist. The news reports bordered on adoration. Writers used such terms as "Pine Bluff Genius," "Wizard of Wonderland," "Pioneer Builder," "Empire Builder," "Human Dynamo," "Couch of Arkansas," and "First Citizen." One writer suggested facetiously that Couch should be made "King of Arkansas." It could have been a heady experience for a former farm boy, but Couch downplayed his achievements as only the results of hard work and belief in the future of the South. He told a Rotary group:

> Our people are now awakening to the new opportunities and a finer spirit of cooperation exists, and I truly believe that during the period from 1925 to 1940 we will see a greater development and expansion than during the period from the Civil War down to 1925...I am glad that I have an opportunity to live in this area and be a part of it.

Couch wanted to become a part of this growth in every way his new-found wealth would allow. On February 10, 1928, he purchased the Louisiana and Arkansas Railroad, valued at over $7 million by the Interstate Commerce Commission. The main line of the railway was 188 miles from Hope, Arkansas (where Couch had seen his first train), to Tioga, Louisiana. By August of the same year he had added the Louisiana Railway and Navigation Company, bringing his system 845 miles of total track. The combined capital of the two companies was placed at over $26 million. Newspapers placed the total value of all the industries Couch now controlled as $200 million.

Couch allowed himself one luxury—Couchwood, a large rustic log cabin built on Lake Catherine. It was in a sense a concrete and log representation of the soul of Harvey Couch. Although he kept his home in Pine Bluff, it was to Couchwood that Couch would bring international bankers, Herbert Hoover, and later Franklin Roosevelt to showcase the best type of living to be found in Arkansas. His finances would have allowed him to build any type of house, anywhere he wanted, but to him Couchwood, with all its simplicity, reflected the best in life. A writer in 1927 had some warm words for Couch's new retreat (but certainly it was not a more enthusiastic description than Couch himself would have used):

> If you should shut your eyes and give free rein to fancy you could not dream a more exquisite lake and hill and woodland picture than Couchwood...Red Cedar logs were shipped from Oregon. The bark was removed and timbers painted...An enormous chimney rose, with it the logs and planks and other things. The spaces between the logs were filled with cement. An inspection will show these things in exquisite harmony. A great porch runs around the south and west sides, and on the east the house drops down to form the first story in which are located the dining room and the kitchen.
>
> There is one great room in the middle of the house and the gazer's eyes are irresistibly drawn to the mammoth fireplace that spans a large portion of the east wall. What glowing logs it will hold this winter!...
>
> Of the eight rooms, three are bedrooms and each has a bath, both tub and shower, hot and cold. The beds are beds which bring sweet dreams. There are closets everywhere and conveniences lurking around to startle you unawares. A trip to the kitchen reveals a large electric range and electric refrigeration. The dining room looks out on the lake that you fancy hides schools of bass and perch.
>
> The big porch is equipped with lounge swings and rustic chairs and is an auxiliary to the bed rooms, where unexpected guests may be put to sleep in the breeze that blows across Lake Catherine. In the big living room... there is an orthophonic Victrola that plays 12 records without quitting, and the polished floor looks good for dancing whether it's ever used for that or not. There is a projector for showing movies and other things. But one of the greatest conveniences that mankind knows is missing and this will appeal to you—there is no telephone there, and we learned that there is not likely to be. Bells are taboo at "Couchwood."

Couch's first guests at his new retreat were his former coworkers on the mail car. Eleven mail clerks, some now on pension, were invited for three days of fishing and relaxation at Couchwood. Couch told reporters that he was appreciative of the encouragement these men had given him when he was an "inexperienced country boy."

A week later Couch entertained Herbert Hoover, on a visit to Arkansas, at Couchwood. Hoover in 1927 was still the Commerce Secretary and was viewing the recovery of flood areas. The final Sunday of Hoover's visit, reporters were allowed into Couchwood to photograph Hoover and Couch. One reporter approached Hoover and asked for a photograph of Hoover fishing on Lake Catherine.

"The Hoovers do not fish on Sunday," Hoover replied.

The photographer persisted. Perhaps Hoover could just pose with a rod and reel?

"The Hoovers do not even pretend to fish on Sunday."

The next year, 1928, Hoover was elected president. He, like Coolidge before him, was reaping the political benefits of the prosperity of the twenties. The stock market seemed to prove Coolidge's adage that the "business of America is business." From September 1924 to February 1926 the Dow Jones Industrials had risen 37 percent. Small investors across the country were using the miracle of leverage buying (buying with loaned money) to take part in the bull market. A new book, *Beating the Stock Market,* was informing the uninitiated how they too could "make $70,000" from their initial investment.

Harvey Couch was not a heavy stock market player, but he was aware of the ride the stock market rocket was giving America. He clipped a small poem from a newspaper and kept it with his personal papers:

Somebody purchased a beautiful yacht,
and will spend the next few months in play
and all on account of a tip he got
on a stock that they call RCA.

But by September 22, 1929, many people were wondering how long the boom could last. An ad in a New York paper headlined "Overstaying A Bull Market" said, "Most investors make money in a bull market, only to lose all the profits made—

92

Pat Neff (center, standing) and Herbert Hoover (seated by door)
at Couchwood

and sometimes more—in the readjustment that inevitably follows." Perhaps this only reflected the thinking of thousands of individual investors, for the market stumbled on October 21, 1929, and did not recover in the days that followed. By October 24, a full-fledged panic was in progress, and over the next few days a series of speculative ups and downs followed, ending in the final crash on October 29, 1929.

Arkansas was not part of the economic mainstream of the country, and at first the Wall Street fiasco seemed like only a Yankee problem. As 1930 developed the main problems in Arkansas involved a summer drought that was ruining the farm crop. Couch was again called on to head the relief effort and again tirelessly marshaled his economic resources to aid the Red Cross relief program. Will Rogers, the comedian, toured Arkansas with Couch giving drought relief benefits and later met with the farmers in each area. At one point Couch turned to see Rogers slipping some money into the hand of one of the farm wives. The two men became close friends; Rogers referred to Couch as his "Arkansas Manager."

Two thousand people attended a stockholders' meeting at the building site of Carpenter Dam in July 1930. None of the speakers of the day mentioned any concern about the value of AP&L stock or the problems on Wall Street. In fact, although the Carpenter Dam project was encountering several delays in construction, the event was the biggest celebration in Arkansas. Radio station KTHS carried the meeting to a state-wide audience. Photographers from the Deluxe Studio in Hot Springs took hundreds of pictures of the crowd and then developed them on-site for distribution that same evening. Music for the event was furnished by the Arkansas Power and Light Orchestra, and a barbeque lunch was served cafeteria style to the thousands who had assembled to hear speeches by Hamilton Moses and Harvey Couch. Couch told both the stockholders and the radio audience that everyone had a stake in the success of Arkansas Power and Light:

> ...A number of years ago I was handicapped in financing by the bad reputation Arkansas had in the East. This has been largely overcome and conditions are much better...
> ...In 1920 the company had only 43 stockholders in Arkansas and now it has 5,800, which is an enormous

Hamilton Moses speaking at Stockholders' Day, July 24, 1930

AP&L Stockholders' Day at Carpenter Dam, July 24, 1930

increase in 10 years. In 1914 the only transmission line in Arkansas was the one between Malvern and Arkadelphia. The state now has 3,000 miles of transmission lines and we are serving nearly every city and village in the state. Besides these we are serving 3,000 farmers carrying the current directly into their homes.

The money expended by the company plays an important part in the finances of the state. Salaries paid to employees in 1930 will amount to $3 million; supplies, most of which are purchased in the state, $4 million; new improvements and developments exclusive of the $7 million being spent on Carpenter Dam, $8 million. The company pays $600,000 in taxes annually, about one-half of which goes to the schools.

At the same time Couch was administering the millions of the Arkansas Power and Light Company, he also was adding more to the drought relief coffers of the state. In January 1931 he worked behind the scenes to end a feud between Hoover and Arkansas Senator Joe T. Robinson about the amount of relief necessary. By February 6 Couch had worked out a deal with Hoover and personally carried the details to Robinson. The next day Robinson approved the compromise, resulting in $20 million in loans to farmers hit by the drought. Newspapers across the country heralded Couch's role as intermediary in the compromise. It was all added to the daily publicity that Couch was now receiving nationwide. *The Magazine of Wall Street,* which had rhetorically asked, "Can anything good come out of Arkansas?" found that yes, indeed, something good could—Harvey Couch.

By the latter part of 1931, Arkansas leaders were much more concerned with the impact the "unemployment situation" was having on the state. Though opinions as to an ultimate cause might differ—one newspaper editorial cartoon laid the blame on "socialist agitators"—everyone agreed that something needed to be done. Almost naturally, Harvey Couch was selected to head the public relief program for the state. However, in the minds of many Arkansans the "unemployment situation" was still secondary to their recovery from the recent drought. On November 26, 1931, Couch addressed Arkansas on a state-wide radio hookup for a Thanksgiving broadcast and observed "nature's bountiful compensation after the 1930 drought."

Most of the construction of Carpenter Dam was nearing

R.E. Elliott of Searcy and another lineman at work, 1931

completion, and the startup date was set for December 1931. The *St. Louis Globe-Democrat* ran a feature in their Sunday Magazine on August 30, showcasing the the new lake resort area of Hot Springs that Carpenter Dam was helping to create.

On October 21, 1931, the lights of Couch's system were dimmed in tribute to Thomas Edison, who was buried that day. Employees observed two minutes of silence in all offices.

By the end of the year the worsening depression made it clear to almost everyone—including Herbert Hoover, who had resisted government involvement in the rebuilding of the economy—that something extraordinary had to be done. On December 7 Hoover's message to Congress outlined a bold new plan:

> In order that the public may be absolutely assured that the Government may be in position to meet any public necessity, I recommend that an emergency Reconstruction Corporation of the nature of the former War Finance Corporation should be established. It may not be necessary to use such an instrumentality very extensively. The very existence of such a bulwark will strengthen confidence…Its purpose is by strengthening the weak spots to thus liberate the full strength of the nation's resources. It should be in position to facilitate exports by American agencies, where necessary to protect and aid the agricultural industry; to make temporary advances upon proper securities to established industries, railways, and financial institutions which otherwise can not secure credit, and where such advances will protect the credit structure and stimulate employment.

A board of seven directors chosen from the ranks of business would lead the new Reconstruction Finance Corporation. These men would automatically become the seven most important businessmen in America, with the ability to give loans and grants that would eventually total hundreds of millions of dollars. Harvey Couch would be one of those seven directors.

Couch jumped at the opportunity to become part of the new giant bureaucracy, although from the beginning he had certain philosophical differences with its chairman, Jesse Jones. The new board was set up mostly to provide large loans to banks and industry. Couch was eager to show the other directors the viewpoint of the "common man."

He felt free to take on this demanding task for several reasons. First, his power companies were now economically stable; Arkansas Power and Light had just announced another price reduction. He kept his role as president of his power companies and train system but had turned the day-to-day activities over to senior management. Also, the demands of family life were less strict now. Harvey's beloved mother, Manie, had died in 1931, and of his children, only Catherine and William remained at home. Judging that the changes in his other responsibilities would allow him to fill the national position as he would like, Couch left for Washington, D.C., and checked into the Mayflower Hotel, where he would reside for the next three years.

By February 1931 the RFC was in operation. Its first loan was to the Bank of America in California, and after that work continued so swiftly that the RFC seemed to be born full-grown. Its Washington offices employed 1,131 and occupied nine floors of an office building. Another 13,093 employees worked in offices across the country. Couch reported to the *Pine Bluff Commercial* that 25,000 entries a day were made in the RFC books.

Requests for money were coming in from across the nation. One of the most memorable came from Bono, Arkansas, and read:

Dear Mr. Couch:

I understand you have something to do with the lending of government money. There are two questions I want to ask you. How much can I get? and When can I get it? Yours truly...

Couch was made supervisor of the public works section of the RFC. This pleased him, since he felt he could use his extensive construction experience in overseeing budgets and encouraging projects that would employ the most workers. Couch would be dispensing monies for water systems, sewage systems, bridges and electric lines in communities across the nation.

In the 1932 election Franklin Roosevelt had displaced Hoover in the White House. Couch was flattered when Roosevelt selected Couch and chairman Jesse Jones as the only Hoover

William, Harvey, Jessie, and Catherine Couch

*Couch and members of the RFC Board presenting report to
President Franklin D. Roosevelt*

appointees to stay on the board when their original two-year term had expired.

Couch continued to work an exhausting number of hours. The RFC was a twelve-hour-day, six-day-a-week occupation. But Couch, who had spent most of his business life trying to acquire money for construction, felt a certain release in now being able to simply distribute money for projects he felt were in the public interest.

Although Couch was working long hours trying to ingratiate himself into the Washington political scene, he made efforts to see that his Arkansas connection remained secure. In preparation for a return visit to Arkansas during Christmas 1932, he wrote with almost paternal concern to his personal secretary, Bill Shepherd, and outlined his plans:

> ...I am thinking that likely I will get to Couchwood Monday night, and on Tuesday night think I would like to invite in all the neighbors and maybe have a big log fire down on the bridge or some place down there and have some little something to eat—a wiener roast and some fruit. Let them bring all their children. And maybe put some kind of entertainment for them. The idea being just because I am away I want them to still feel that I am interested in them and like to have them come to see me...

Couch had a variety of tasks on the RFC Board. He sat in on hearings on prosposed projects and sometimes initiated and organized the presentations of projects that fell within his sphere of interest. Although it is difficult to trace single projects to any one board member, Couch was viewed as responsible for several of the largest construction projects undertaken by the RFC during its first years.

He helped supporters of a San Franciso–Oakland bridge organize their proposal for the board meeting. He then actively promoted it and answered the objections of other board members.

When Huey P. Long objected to a proposed New Orleans bridge, Couch met with Long to try to overcome his objections. Couch used an old sales technique and offered to name the bridge the Huey P. Long Bridge. Long dropped his objections.

Couch also worked on several projects for the Los Angeles area. He oversaw plans for funneling water from the Colorado River to Los Angeles and a transmission line from Hoover Dam to the city.

Though proud of his and the RFC's work to help the nation recover from the depression, Couch was still dissatisfied with the restraints built into the RFC work. Couch wanted government programs to be available to what he called the "grass roots" of American workers. As the depression worsened, it became clear that the large-scale projects of the RFC were not reaching the number of workers that needed to be helped. When the WPA was established in 1933, its duties were to fund the type of small-scale projects—schools, roads, and other civic improvements—that Couch had originally envisioned. To a great extent this would eclispe some of his duties with the RFC, so Couch decided to step away from that organization. Couch sent his resignation to Roosevelt but stayed on at Roosevelt's request so that the first days of the WPA would go smoothly. Roosevelt finally accepted Couch's resignation on August 16, 1934. Couch took 1,400 employees of the RFC on a "farewell cruise" along the Potomac. A band played dance music while the guests were served Couch's favorite food—hot dogs. News services from across the country carried photos of the excursion along with captions that proclaimed, "Hot Dogs Get Into Society."

From his first days at the RFC Board Couch had brought a different perspective to a government with a largely urban viewpoint. His ideas on how to end the depression came from his background in the South. Sometimes northern newspapers found that Couch's Arkansas background made good copy, as when Couch won a hog-calling contest on a visit back to Arkansas; but on other occasions his ideas must have been comprehensible only to southerners or farmers. In 1931 he suggested:

...We believe the most certain safeguard is a nationwide back to the soil movement. I do not have in mind the thought that great masses of people would move from urban communities to the rural sections and enter into competition with the farmer—and I cannot stress this too strongly—but that the wage earner employed in the city and town would make his home in the country on a place of two, five or even ten acres. I refer to the worker in the factory, in the business house, in an office, or on the railroad, a mechanic or a worker in the building trades who of necessity is employed intermittently. Instead of occupying a house on a cramped 50-foot lot in town his home would be on a small tract of land a few miles from the city. In this day of good roads and almost universal ownership of motor cars, his residence would be as near the scene of his employment as it was ten years ago when he lived only a few blocks distant.

On his home place he would have a cow and poultry, perhaps two or three hogs, and the means for producing cheaply the food with which to maintain them. He would have a few fruit trees, a garden as a source of fresh vegetables, some rows of potatoes, and so on, and his kitchen would be equipped with a pressure cooker and sealer to put up canned food and preserves for use during the winter. His backyard, so to speak, would provide a living for his family and himself the year round, releasing for other purposes cash which otherwise would go for foodstuffs...

Couch's emphasis on a land-based recovery from the depression remained constant even upon his meeting with Roosevelt on the day of his resignation. Couch recited a poem he had made up which he thought might encourage people to take a more aggressive attitude toward working their way out of the depression. It ran:

A garden and a sow,
A smokehouse and a cow,
Twenty-four hens and a rooster,
And you'll have more than you uster.

Roosevelt asked if he could write the poem down. He wanted to include it in his next speech. It was a poetic farewell to Washington political life for Harvey Couch.

Chapter Seven

COUCH WANTED TO return to Arkansas for several reasons. First, in 1934 he was 57 years old. The fires of ambition still burned brightly inside him, but he was more aware of the rush of time. Harvey Couch still had more that he wanted to accomplish.

His most important unrealized goal centered on rural electrification. Couch had told Franklin Roosevelt that he wanted the government to help support private companies in their attempts to make the building of lines to isolated farms affordable. The Reconstruction Finance Corporation was now providing funds to the Rural Electrification Administration to do just that for public projects. Couch had always felt a bond with farmers and now he strongly wanted to be the man to bring electricity to the farm. His sense of urgency was based more on his identification with farmers than on the amount of money the scattered customers would bring his utility.

The expense of connecting farmers to transmission lines had delayed rural electrification across the country. Now that the government was funding electrification projects and co-ops, a widespread movement was underway to assert government control over all aspects of the nation's electric utilities. This thought horrified Harvey Couch. Although only a few people were espousing full government control, Couch knew that this movement could spread quickly if private electric utilities did not prove themsleves to the public. An effective rural electrification program could be viewed as a matter of corporate survival.

With Couch's return in August 1934, he began two projects that would carry his attention for the remainder of his business life. First, he assigned AP&L's electrical superintendent Ralph Pittman the job of devising a new type of electrical distribution system that would make it easier to bring electricity to the farm—something cheaper than what was then in place but still safe as an electrical transmission system.

The second plan was more philosophical but, Couch thought, still practical for the future of Arkansas. Couch's terms as RFC director had widened his view of the American economic system. By working directly with northern banks and large manufacturing concerns he had discovered what he felt was a basic weakness in Arkansas's economy.

Arkansas was a state rich in resources; water, cotton, rice, timber, and other agricultural products were the basis of the state's wealth. However, being only a resource provider would be forever limiting to a sound economic base. Companies that actually processed those resources determined pricing and payments. Couch was referred to as a "voice in the wilderness" by a Memphis *Commercial Appeal* reporter who recounted Couch's address to a civic club this way:

> All his life Mr. Couch, like the rest of us, has heard orators expatiate upon the vast natural resources of Arkansas. He has heard Arkansas described in glowing terms as "The Wonder State." He has heard it said, and knows full well on his own authority, that the state contains a bountiful supply of nearly all the useful metals known to science and industry. He knows its soil from the rich alluvial valleys to the top of its barren Ozark Mountains, its fields and streams, fish and fowl... Knowing all of these things from his youth up, he is wondering why something has not been done about it.
>
> Mr. Couch assumes that the poets and orators have done about all that is necessary to immortalize the possibilities and hidden resources of the state. He has an idea that they should be brought to light and made useful. For example, there is nothing particularly poetic about the suggestion, but it is characteristic and intensely practical that he should urge the manufacture of plow lines.
>
> Arkansas's cotton crop amounts to 1,000,000 bales.

All of it shipped out of state, manufactured into useful articles, shipped back and sold. Plow lines, he tells a Little Rock luncheon, are manufactured from low grade cotton, costing six or eight cents a pound. The rope is sold for 20 and 30 cents a pound. That state that produces the raw product could also manufacture the finished product and the one industry alone would mean an additional $500,000 [to the state's economy] a year...

The suggestions that Couch made continued along the same unglamourous lines and received little press attention. But Couch believed that the business future of Arkansas depended on the development of small industries. He did not think heavy manufacturing would ever come to the state, but developing simple, small-scale production facilties would make a greater impact on the state than trying to attract a northern manufacturer to locate there.

By the end of 1934, Ralph Pittman and his crew had designed a new type of transmission wire that revolutionized rural electrification. The new line utilized only one insulated wire and one grounded neutral. Although this technique could have been patented, Couch turned the design over to the REA for use in rural electrification across the country and in other countries around the world. The simple rural line concept lowered construction costs from $1,500 a mile to $750 a mile. Immediately Couch sent the first crew to connect to his system an area including Magnet Cove and Prattsville, which only had five customers to the mile. The system was connected on February 22, 1935, and the NBC radio network carried a coast-to-coast broadcast of the electrification ceremonies. Couch's son Harvey Jr. substituted for Couch, who had fallen off a horse at Couchwood and was recovering there. Congratulations wired by Franklin Roosevelt were read to the nationwide audience.

Meanwhile Couch continued an earlier system that allowed farmers to work with crews to bring the lines to their farms and help reduce costs. In payment he would accept chickens, eggs, cattle, or anything of value that depression-plagued farmers could afford.

With the new rural electrification procedure, Couch was able to increase the pace of bringing power to the farmers of his service area. By 1937 AP&L's rural electrification program called for completion of 4,055 miles of new lines to 16,634 farms. On October 31, 1937, the *Arkansas Gazette* carried a report in its Sunday Magazine section on how electricity had changed the farm:

> John Jones, an Arkansas farmer of average means, is awakened early one bright fall morning by the ringing of his electric alarm clock.
> Dressing leisurely, he starts for his cow barn, stopping on the way to flip on the switch that starts his electric water pump.
> Arrived at the barn, he goes through the routine of attaching the electric milking machine to first one cow, then another, until his herd of nine are all milked.
> Placing the foaming milk in an electric cooler, he steps into an adjoining room to shell the corn for his hogs in an electric sheller. Then he dumps the ingredients for his mixed feed into an electric mixer...
> Outside he takes the portable motor he has used to operate the corn huller and the feed mixer, and moves it over to a wood saw. In a few minutes he has enough wood cut to last for the rest of the week ...

Since Couch's rural electrification projects were running at full capacity, he now felt he could return to his new favorite subject— the development of the Arkansas economy. Speaking before civic groups Couch repeated how Arkansas could take control of its own economic fate:

> ...Industrial development is achieved by processing or manufacturing articles to a finished state for consumption.
> Essentials are accessible raw products...What are raw products, and how should we utilize them?
> There is lumber. This should go into furniture, radio cabinets, wagons, and other finished articles.
> Cotton should be made into clothing, shorts, dresses, stockings, sheeting, etc., right here at home.
> Sand—glass, bottles, and other articles.
> Bauxite—aluminum and aluminum products...

The list continued, but Couch's audience was getting the idea. To help encourage action, Couch repeated a strategy he had used earlier to help sell Arkansas. He brought investors, this time from around the world, to visit him at Couchwood and to meet Arkansas businessmen—hoping that fiscal lightning might strike.

The newspapers carried monthly accounts of the visitors who could mean business for the state. "Arkansas Business Leaders will meet New York Financier," "International Banker Visits State," "Business Men Greet John M. Schiff," "Eastern Financier is Guest at Couchwood." Couch, remembering his early difficulties in finding sufficient capital to finance his dream, was sensitive to the needs of Arkansas businessmen with their own dreams. He seemed to have no trouble bringing financiers to Arkansas to meet with local businessmen by offering them the pleasures of country life in return. He provided a program (with a portrait of the invited guest on the front cover) for each of the visits. The program gives a good indication of what everyone expected. A typical program for Clarence Dillon read:

Open Letter to Couchwood Guests:

1. When you come into the big gate, forget all your troubles (if any).
2. Be sure to sign the register. Couchwood is proud of its guests.
3. At meals take as many helpings as you desire.
4. If you don't see what you want, ask for it (just like you would at home). At Couchwood everything is off the record.

The program listed the following agenda:

SHAKING HANDS
HAVING A GOOD TIME
EATING
AND THE MAGNOLIA SQUARE DANCERS

A typical menu included baked chicken and Couch's beloved hot dogs. The visits were simple, but Couch thought that the simplicity of the Arkansas life style would be attractive to

New York bankers on railroad tour of Arkansas

An evening's entertainment at Couchwood—dancing to records played on the Victrola

Couch entertaining dinner guests at Couchwood

A baseball game at Camp Couchdale near Couchwood: Harvey Couch catching and Postmaster General James A. Farley batting

Harvey Couch (seated at center) with businessmen guests at Couchwood

these high-powered businessmen. He was not, however, above pulling the legs of each of his sophisticated visitors. As it grew dark at these outdoor dinners Couch would take the current guest aside and point out the fires from imaginary corn stills which Couch claimed were being operated at night in the hills across from Couchwood. Invariably, after a little squinting and straining, the guest of honor would say that yes, he could just make them out. The Arkansas businessmen held their tongues as they chewed on their hot dogs.

But along with the good times at Couchwood, a realistic Couch tried to insure that each of his guests carried away more than fond memories of Arkansas life. He wanted them to see the potential for investment. A schedule of a "side trip" for business-men on their way to Couchwood provides some insight into Couch's main purpose for the visits.

> Program—March 4: Arrive at Springhill [La.] 7 a.m. Calls to be made at that time. Breakfast. Inspection of Mill. En route to Minden [La.] stop at United Gas Company's compress station and see deep oil tests. Arrive at Minden in time to depart at 10 a.m. Note: Pine Bluff will provide two cars. Truck to bring baggage from Springhill to Couchwood...Depart from Minden at 10 a.m. and arrive at Sterlington at 12 noon. Inspect United Gas Company compression station and powerhouse. Luncheon in the company boardinghouse. Depart for Crossett via Bastop at 1:15 and arrive at Crossett at 2:15. View forestry exhibit. Depart for El Dorado at 2:45, arriving at 3:45. Hurried trip to Schuler oil field, returning to El Dorado by 5 p.m. Depart for Couchwood via Camden, reaching Couch-wood at 7 p.m. Supper at 7:30. Note: C.P. (Pete) Couch to arrange for motorcycle police to assure prompt move-ment while in Louisiana; see that Governor is provided with car to make trip from Minden to Sterlington and wherever else he wishes to go in order to arrive at Alexan-dria [La.] Saturday morning...Harvey Couch to provide motorcycle policemen in Arkansas.

Couch continued his public service during the last half of the 1930s. In 1936 he served as the state's Centennial Chairman. He invited Roosevelt to attend the ceremonies and hosted him during his stay in the state. Couch continued to be a strong

Harvey Couch and family standing in front of old family home in Calhoun, 1932

The Harvey Couch family, fall 1933: (back row, left to right) Harvey, Jr., Johnson Olin, Kirke, (front row, left to right) William, Jessie, Harvey, Catherine

Harvey Couch Day in Pine Bluff, around 1933

Roosevelt supporter even though the spectre of government power continued to rise under Roosevelt's leadership. The TVA was becoming the government's large-scale foray into public power in neighboring Tennessee. Couch also was dealing with another threat when the Utility Holding Act broke up the nation's larger utility holding companies. Electric Bond and Share was one of those companies, and Arkansas Power and Light, Mississippi Power and Light, and Louisiana Power and Light would be spun off into a separate entity, which would eventually become Middle South Utilities.

Couch tried to keep the public power agitators at bay by pledging to keep his system's utility rates at the same level as that of the new Tennessee Valley Authority project—two cents per kilowatt-hour. He also began to initiate plans for the third dam on the Ouachita River. For this dam he hoped to get some of the bonds now available for electric generation construction, so he dropped the original plans to name the dam after himself and chose the name of nearby Blakely Mountain. In the press he began to promote the idea that private utilities could match or beat any program that the government could develop.

Couch kept moving with his railroad plans as well. Beginning in 1937, he started acquiring stock in the Kansas City Southern, which was in financial trouble. Couch won an agreement with the Amsterdam bankers who had taken over the railroad, and by 1938 he assumed control of the KCS and the next year combined it with his Louisiana and Arkansas Company. The merger gave him a system that stretched from New Orleans to Kansas City.

Immediately, he began an overhaul of the aging system. He bought new cars from the Pullman Company, ordering them to purchase their materials for the cars from within the Kansas City Southern service area. He also acquired new oil-electric engines that would increase the speed of each train. Couch rode a well-publicized "speed test" from Kansas City to Texarkana where the average speed was clocked at 56 miles per hour.

Later that same year, 1939, he amazed the rail industry by announcing he would develop a combined air-rail-motor transportation system that would follow the routes of the Kansas City Southern. Couch wanted one for all types of passenger and freight transportation in the South. With lightning speed Couch

(Left to right) Harvey Couch, Senator Hattie Caraway, Senator Joe T. Robinson, and Vice President John Nance Garner with Arkansas centennial coin

(Left to right, standing) Senator Hattie Caraway, Harvey Couch, and Senator Joe T. Robinson presenting Arkansas centennial half-dollar to President Roosevelt, January 27, 1936

acquired government approval for his plan, and the first three airplanes for the system.

Couch was pushing frantically to develop an empire that would have sapped his energy even as a young man. Now he was in his sixties. He celebrated his sixty-second birthday in his office at Pine Bluff. Couch knew that in different times there would be tremendous opposition for his almost monopolistic transportation system. But the depression had ruined the rail industry and Couch's efforts were singular in trying to develop a new type of rail system for the new times. As rail stock became almost valueless, Couch continued to invest heavily in other rail companies.

In February 1940, Couch developed a bad case of the flu. He had not recovered when he attended the Democratic Convention that would renominate Franklin Roosevelt in Chicago. As a strong supporter of Jesse Jones, who was running against Henry Wallace for the vice-presidency, Couch felt compelled to go.

Couch was disappointed when Wallace was selected and flew on to close a business deal in Baltimore. In a barber shop in that city, he suffered a mild heart attack and was checked into a hospital. Couch's family came to Washington and stayed with him while he recuperated. In a master stroke of public relations, Couch kept the severity of his health problems hidden from the public.

When he returned to Arkansas he went directly to Couchwood where it was announced he was recovering from a "recent illness." The press, which knew of the extent of that illness, cooperated by printing vague doctor reports which stated that Couch was expected back at work in after a few weeks of well-deserved rest.

Jessie Couch, who had spent her life in the shadow of her husband, now stepped forward and began answering his correspondence. She responded to one letter:

> ...I'm happy to tell you that Harvey seems to have begun to improve. Still restricting visitors, but he does see some of the departmental heads of AP&L & of course his brother Pete...

Harvey Couch with a day's catch at Couchwood

Still later she would answer another letter:

> ...Harvey is still not able to write, but his appetite yet calls for apples, so he wants to thank you for remembering and especially something that he can eat now.
> We are hoping his dearly beloved Couchwood with its pure air, no noise and favorite servants will soon start him on the road back to recovery.

Looking at news accounts of the period at the beginning of 1941, no one would suspect that Harvey Couch was so seriously ill. He was director of the state Polio Campaign while stationed at Couchwood. Hamilton Moses was assuming all of Couch's work-related chores and protecting him from any of the strains that went with them. The press knew that Harvey Couch would not recover, but the question that was on each of their minds was: How long could he last?

This point created a symbiotic relationship between the Couch family and the press. They would not print any stories that accurately portrayed the extent of his illness, but in return the Couch family provided space on their grounds, including sleeping arrangements, for reporters who made the trek down to Couchwood.

Harvey Couch was certainly an optimist. His entire life had been one of optimistic risk-taking. But he could not be hopeful as one doctor after another could not seem to find an answer for his worsening heart disease. Although he had visitors, and sometimes an occasional photograph would appear in the papers, Harvey Couch was an exhausted man.

As his health continued to worsen, Couch was ordered by his doctor to move into another cabin on the Couchwood property that had air conditioning. An annex was built on the small cabin to make room for the staff of doctors and nurses that were there on a 24-hour basis. Couch was immobile, but his mind continued to run at full speed. He ordered another cabin to be built nearby for his newly married daughter Catherine and her husband Pratt Remmel. The cabin, originally intended to face the lake, was turned toward Couch's cabin so that he could watch construction. Each morning, nurses would gently lead him to a rocking chair, which had a headrest attached for the purpose, so that he could watch his last construction project near completion. Eventually, even this became too much of a strain on his weakening heart.

When Couch heard of the death of W.E. Baker, a business associate and friend since the first days of his telephone company, the future, for the first time, looked bleak. He turned to Jessie with tears in his eyes and said, "That breaks my heart." He was right. On July 30, 1941, he died in his sleep—with some dreams, as always, unfinished. The reporters camped on the grounds of Couchwood raced to wire the news across the country. One writer had access to Couch's own arrangements for his funeral. Couch had begun his final declaration with the statement, "Whatever I am belongs to my family and Arkansas."

Index

126